武汉纺织大学学术著作出版基金资助出版

EFFICIENT CHINESE LEARNING THROUGH CULTURAL IMMERSION

文化浸入式
国际汉语高效教程

主　编◎吴　卉
副主编◎谭燕保　林　莉　柯群胜

華中科技大學出版社
http://www.hustp.com
中国·武汉

图书在版编目(CIP)数据

文化浸入式国际汉语高效教程/吴卉主编. —武汉:华中科技大学出版社,2020.12
ISBN 978-7-5680-6723-2

Ⅰ.①文… Ⅱ.①吴… Ⅲ.①汉语-对外汉语教学-教材 Ⅳ.①H195.4

中国版本图书馆 CIP 数据核字(2020)第 250401 号

文化浸入式国际汉语高效教程 吴 卉 主编
Wenhua Jinrushi Guoji Hanyu Gaoxiao Jiaocheng

策划编辑:刘 平 兰 刚
责任编辑:刘 平
责任校对:封力煊
封面设计:原色设计
责任监印:周治超
出版发行:华中科技大学出版社(中国·武汉) 电话:(027)81321913
武汉市东湖新技术开发区华工科技园 邮编:430223
录 排:华中科技大学出版社美编室
印 刷:武汉开心印印刷有限公司
开 本:787mm×1092mm 1/16
印 张:18 插页:2
字 数:343 千字
版 次:2020 年 12 月第 1 版第 1 次印刷
定 价:58.00 元

前　　言

《文化浸入式国际汉语高效教程》是特别为非汉语专业的外国留学生量身定制的，目的是让他们在快速学习汉语的同时了解中国文化，领略中国古代圣贤的智慧结晶。本教材分为四个模块。

第一模块：拼音（基础知识、发音练习）；

第二模块：汉字（基础知识、汉字分类）；

第三模块：中华文化经典（古文、古诗词、传统节日）；

第四模块：课文（对话、短文）。

编者对本教材进行了深入的思考和调研，历经多年探索和尝试，做了如下改革创新。

一、分模块系统学习

第一步直接进入语音模块。在此阶段不穿插课文、生词等内容，而是直接把整个汉语拼音的框架介绍给留学生。在大框架下，学生全面学习所有内容，包括声母、韵母、整体认读音节、发音规则、特殊情况等，然后立即进入到有意义的发音练习中。

可能有人会质疑，这么快把众多拼音知识教授给学生，他们会不会接受不了？答案是不会。大部分留学生来中国之前就已经学过拼音了，即便他们是零基础拼音，也不会成为障碍。因为他们精通英语，自然会对拉丁化的汉语拼音有较高的接受度，学起来很快。再者，对于成年人来说，系统的总结归纳性教学法最适合他们。

第二步进入汉字模块，开门见山地教他们如何写字。为什么不在课文中穿插如何写字呢？答案还是不够全面系统。我们的教学对象是成年人，教学方法自然与教小孩不同，需要更多归纳总结性的知识。汉字作为图形文字，对于习惯字母文字的外国人来说是个极大的难点。在教学中穿插一点如何写字的讲解，是不全面，也显得不够重要的。所谓磨刀不误砍柴工，在学习课文之前先全面了解写字的方法及意义，对之后的课文学习将大有帮助，效率也会大大提高。

第三步进入中华文化经典模块。语言和文化学习相互助力，相得益彰，此部分也着重体现了本书的文化浸入式特点，让留学生在学习语言的过程中，被我们古代圣贤的智慧、精神所熏陶和感染，从而接受中华文化，并对其产生浓厚的兴趣。

第四步进入课文模块。此部分根据留学生在中国实际生活、学习的情况，模拟真实语言场景设计，如银行开户、滴滴打车等，都是他们最需要掌握的语言实际应用知识与技能。这部分回归常规的教学模式，从课文、生词、练习等方面展开。因为之前已全面系统地学习和练习过拼音、汉字，所以到课文部分就会轻松不少，进度也会比较快。

二、文化浸入式学习

整本教材在文化的烘托下展开，文化语境从古典文学到日常生活，让初学者了解中国古代文化的渊源，感受它的博大精深，也了解当代中国生活的活力，激发他们的学习兴趣。

语音阶段的常规做法是用简单无意义的拼音练习发音。编者改变了传统做法，将拼音练习的内容改为中国古典文化代表作，如《弟子规》《三字经》等。有人可能会问：这么难的东西恐怕连中国学生都搞不明白，外国人怎么可能学会？回答是不用现在懂，只要读。因为这里只是练习发音而已，不需要彻底明白其中的含义。那又会有人问，只是练习发音为什么要用这些内容呢，别的不行吗？当然行，但是这些内容更好，因为它们是中华文化的瑰宝，流传千年，朗朗上口，简单押韵，集趣味性及知识性于一体，更加有利于发音练习。当学生尝试去解读这些文字的时候，他们其实就已经开始了解中国古人凝练的智慧了。在以后的日子里，当他们顿悟一些人生的道理，回过头来看这些文字时，就会感叹中国古人之伟大。

汉字阶段主要围绕文化进行，因为汉字本身就具有文化内涵。象形、指事、形声、会意、转注、假借等都是运用了中国智慧的造字法，所以在介绍汉字类型和书写方法的时候，文化的内容就自然而然被带入了。中国文字博大精深，是打开中华文化的钥匙，外国人必须用很多时间和精力来攻克这个难关。

课文阶段既有中国文化，也涉及现代生活，比如讲旅游主题的时候会介绍中国的名山大川，讲美食主题的时候会介绍中国特色的美味佳肴。

三、针对非汉语专业外国留学生

对于非汉语专业的留学生来说，他们的中文课很少，而且科目单一。如何利用课堂有限的时间来提高他们的汉语水平，这是一个值得研究的课题。

经过调研，我们发现教授非汉语专业留学生学习汉语可以采取如下方式。

第一，留学生大多为热爱学术的优秀青年，他们已经形成了一定的知识体系，有较强的理解力和自学能力。教师可以用比较快的速度，比较系统的方法给他们上课，充分利用有限的课时量，最大限度地给他们多讲授有价值的知识。课堂只是“师傅领进门”，“修行靠个人”就是课下自学了。自学效果可以用平时成绩来约束，教师可以通过加大作业量，增加课堂测试次数等来督促学生学习。

第二，教师要有针对性，比如详细的语法、地道的发音等都无须花太多课时，因为即便当时花很多时间去纠正发音，母语的影响也是很难改变的。留学生最需要的是高效学会实用性知识，因此无须在语言学的专业性上要求过多。教师在设计教程时应该控制好比重，突出侧重点，选择有针对性、对他们更有用的材料。

第三，外国留学生具有各种宗教背景。中国是一个没有传统宗教的国家，我国现存的宗教，如佛教、伊斯兰教、基督教、天主教等都是从国外传入的。道教从严格意义上来讲，不是宗教信仰，而是中国古人在探索追寻宇宙和人的关系，不具有排他性的意识形态，只是中国古人思考和智慧的结晶。所以，向外国留学生宣传中国儒家思想的包容性，是必不可少的。否则，语言失去了外界对自己文化的接纳，就是空洞无根源的。

第四，留学生的英语大都很好，所以与国际音标比较近似的拼音对于他们来说并不难。在全面介绍完拼音规则之后，使用朗朗上口、有节奏有韵律的文本来练习发音是再好不过了。《弟子规》《三字经》这样的文化经典用于练习发音能起到一举多得的作用。既能练习发音，也能接触儒家思想，了解中国文化。这个时候如果使用单字、二字词、三字词这样简单又无意义的内容来练习发音是很浪费时间的。对于非汉语专业的留学生来说，应该着眼于如何在有限的时间里让他们学到更多的实用知识，操练及延伸性的东西应该留给课外。

随着中国崛起，中国和中国文化又一次引起了西方的关注。在"一带一路"倡议下，汉语和中国文化推广有许多工作可做。编者在对外汉语教学的岗位上工作几年后发现，教授外国人汉语，在国内环境下和国外环境下，情况完全不同；对于汉语专业和非汉语专业的留学生，教学方法也不能一样；教不同年龄段的人，方法也不尽相同。教学法当然可以互相借鉴，但教学效果更取决于个性。英语在世界上已经传播了一两百年，在教学方面积累了丰富的经验和方法。中文在真正意义上走向世界虽然已有三十余年，但只能说才刚刚起步，特别是教学法上还未摆脱英语的影响。这方面的研究大有潜力可挖，而且前景非常广阔。

不仅如此，国家提出要"文化自信"，这让大学英语课程都开始将普及中国文化当作重头戏，更何况对外汉语教学是面向众多外国人，是汉语言文化传播最直接且重要的途径。改革开放后，特别是进入21世纪以来，随着中国由"本土型国家"转变为"国际型国家"，"文化强国"和"中国文化走出去"成为重大的国家战略。传播中国文化之重要性无须赘述，应当不遗余力地增强国家语言文化实力，传播中华文化，促进各国人民之间的广泛交往。作为教育工作者，我们必须为之不断努力、改革创新，不断探索更为科学、更加行之有效的教学方法。

由于时间及水平有限，书中难免出现各种错误和问题，敬请专家和使用者匡正并谅解。感谢！

吴　卉

2020 年 8 月

目　录

Part One Syllables

1.1 Basic Knowledge

1.1.1 What Are Chinese Syllables

The Chinese language is composed of Chinese Pinyin and Chinese Characters. Chinese characters are the writing symbols of the Chinese language. Pinyin is the phonetics for Chinese characters. Pinyin tells us how to pronounce. There are 26 letters in Chinese Phonetic Alphabet.

汉语由汉语拼音和汉字组成。汉字是汉语的书写符号，拼音则是汉字的注音符号。拼音教我们如何发音。汉语拼音字母表里有 26 个字母。

They are:

如下：

A ɑ	B b	C c	D d	E e	F f	G g
H h	I i	J j	K k	L l	M m	N n
O o	P p	Q q	R r	S s	T t	
U u	V v	W w	X x	Y y	Z z	

They look like the English letters, but V is only used to spell loanwords, minority languages and dialects.

拼音字母与英语字母相似，但是 V 只用来拼写外来语、少数民族语言和方言。

Chinese pinyin is the basis of recognition and pronunciation for Chinese characters, the cornerstone of learning Mandarin, and the tool for reading and writing.

汉语拼音是认读汉字字音的基础，是学习普通话的基石，也是阅读写作的工具。

Chinese Syllables consist of three parts：the initial，the final and the tone.

拼音包括三个部分：声母、韵母和声调。

Such as：

如下：

Syllables（Pinyin）	Parts	Explanation
mā	m	the initial
	a	the final
	—	the tone（other tones：má mǎ mà ma）

1.1.2 Initials

Initials are the consonant(s) at the beginning of the syllable. The initial can be one letter as well as two letters.

声母是位于音节开头的辅音。声母可以是一个字母，也可以是两个字母。

Such as：

如下：

Syllables	Initials
bà	b
guāng	g
chí	ch
zhuǎi	zh

In Chinese syllables，there are 23 initials.

在汉语拼音中，有 23 个声母。

Such as：

如下：

b p m f
d t n l
g k h
j q x
zh ch sh r
z c s
y w

In certain cases, there are no initials. Sometimes, there are only finals and tones.

特殊情况下,没有声母。有时只有韵母和声调。

These are the most used in Mandarin:

以下是普通话中常用的:

ā(吖) á(嗄) ǎ(啊) à(呵) ɑ(阿)
āi(埃) ái(皑) ǎi(矮) ài(艾)
ān(安) ǎn(俺) àn(岸)
āng(肮) áng(昂) àng(盎)
āo(凹) áo(熬) ǎo(袄) ào(奥)
ē(婀) é(俄) ě(恶) è(扼) e(呃)
ēi(欸,express "hello":~,你快来!)
éi(欸,express "surprised":~,你怎么哭了?)
ěi(欸,express "don't agree":~,这你就错了。)
èi(欸,express "agree":~,我马上过来。)
ēn(恩) èn(摁)
ér(儿) ěr(耳) èr(二)

ō(噢,express "understand":～,原来是他!)

ó(哦,express "doubt":～,她也要来?)

ǒ(哦,express "surprised":～,你们也去呀?)

ò(哦,express "suddenly understand":～,我懂了。)

ōu(欧)　ǒu(呕)　òu(沤)

1.1.3 Finals

The final is the latter part of a syllable. The final can be one letter (which is called a single final) as well as two or more than two letters (which is called a compound final).

韵母是拼音的后部分。韵母可以是一个字母(称为单韵母),也可以是二个或多个字母(称为复韵母)。

Such as:

如下:

Syllables	Finals
měng	eng
pǒ	o
shuài	uai

In fact, there are only 24 finals used frequently. They are:

事实上,我们频繁使用的韵母只有 24 个,它们是:

a	o	e	i	u	ü			
ai	ei	ui	ao	ou	iu	ie	üe	er
an	en	in	un	ün	ang	eng	ing	ong

Meanwhile, in Chinese syllables, some are composed of two frequently used finals. There are 35 finals in total. They all include one or more vowels: *a*,*o*,*e*,*i*,*u*,*ü*.

在汉语拼音中,还有一些韵母由两个常用韵母组合而成。韵母共有 35 个,它们都包含一个或几个元音字母 a、o、e、i、u、ü。

Such as:

如下:

	i	u	ü
a	ia	ua	
o		uo	
e	ie		üe
ai		uai	
ei		ui	
ao	iao		
ou	iou		
an	ian	uan	üan
en	in	un	ün
ang	iang	uang	
eng	ing	ueng	
ong	iong		

NOTES:

① If you want to use the final "i" to form a Chinese syllable whose former part doesn't have any initial, you should write the syllable like *yi*, *ya*, *ye*, *yao*, *you*, *yan*, *yin*, *yang*, *ying* or *yong*. Because the pronunciation of "y" = "i".

i 列的韵母,前面没有声母的时候,写成 yi、ya、ye、yao、you、yan、yin、yang、ying 或 yong。

② If you want to use the final "u" to form a Chinese syllable whose former part doesn't have any initial, you should write the syllable like *wu*, *wa*, *wo*, *wai*, *wei*, *wan*, *wen*, *wang* or *weng*. Because the pronunciation of "w"="u".

u 列的韵母,前面没有声母的时候,写成 wu、wa、wo、wai、wei、wan、wen、wang 或 weng。

③ If you want to use the final "ü" to form a Chinese syllable whose former part doesn't have any initial, you should write the syllable like *yu*, *yue*, *yuan* or *yun*. All in all, you should remove the two dots above the "ü" in this situation. Because the pronunciation of "yu" = " ü ".

ü 列的韵母，前面没有声母的时候，写成 yu、yue、yuan 或 yun。简而言之，此情况下 ü 上两点省略。

④ "ü" is a special vowel sound. If you want to use the final "ü" to form a Chinese syllable whose initial is *j*, *q*, *x* or *y*, you have to remove the two dots above the "ü", such as: *jú*, *qǔ*, *xū*, *yú*. But, if you want to use the final "ü" to form a Chinese syllable whose initial is *n* or *l*, you have to keep the two dots above the "ü", such as: *lǘ*, *nǚ*.

ü 是一个特殊的元音。ü 行的韵母跟声母 j，q，x 拼的时候，ü 上两点省略，如：jú，qǔ，xū。但是，跟声母 n，l 拼的时候，保留 ü 上两点，如：lǘ，nǚ。

⑤ When add initials before *iou*, *uei* or *uen*, you should cancel the middle letter, so change *iou* into *iu*, *uei* into *ui*, and *uen* into *un*. Here are some examples: *n*＋*iou*＝*niu*, *g*＋*uei*＝*gui*, *l*＋*uen*＝*lun*.

iou，uei，uen 前面加声母的时候，去掉中间的字母写成 iu，ui，un。例如，n＋iou＝niu（牛），g＋uei ＝gui（归），l＋uen ＝lun（抡）。

Finals follow the initial. Finals can be classified into two types: **Simple Finals** and **Compound Finals** (including **Finals with a Nasal Ending**).

韵母位于声母之后，分为单韵母和复韵母（包括鼻韵母）。

Single Finals contain only one final.

单韵母仅由一个韵母组成。

There are six single finals.

单韵母有六个。

They are all vowels:

他们都是元音：

a	o	e	i	u	ü

Compound Finals are composed of two or three finals.

复韵母由两到三个韵母组成。

There are fourteen compound finals in two letters.

两个字母组成的复韵母有十四个。

They are:

他们是:

ai	ei	ui
ao	ou	iu
ie	üe	er
an	en	in
un	ün	

There are four compound finals in three letters.

三个字母组成的复韵母有四个。

They are:

他们是:

ang	eng	ing	ong

There are nine finals with nasal sound. Five finals are with front nasal sound and four finals are with back nasal sound. They are:

有九个鼻音韵母,其中五个是前鼻韵,四个是后鼻韵。他们是:

Front Nasal Finals	an	en	in	un	ün
Back Nasal Finals	ang	eng	ing	ong	

1.1.4 Tones

Mandarin has four tones. They are the first tone, the second tone, the third tone and the fourth tone.

普通话有四个声调。他们是一声(阴平)、二声(阳平)、三声(上声)、四声(去声)。

Such as:

如下:

ā á ǎ à	ō ó ǒ ò
ē é ě è	ī í ǐ ì
ū ú ǔ ù	ǖ ǘ ǚ ǜ

Simply speaking, when writing Pinyin, the tone mark is usually placed above the stressed vowel.

简单来说,书写拼音时,我们通常把声调标注在重读的元音上面。

But there are specific rules. They are:

但是还是有明确的规则。如下:

① If the final has only one vowel letter, just mark the tone above the vowel letter.

韵母为单个元音字母时,声调就标在该元音字母上面。

Such as:

如下:

mǐ ān tǔ

② If the final has several vowel letters, mark the tone above the vowel letter according to the order of *a*, *o*, *e*, *i*, *u*, *ü*.

韵母为多个元音字母时,按 a、o、e、i、u、ü 的顺序,声调标在最前面的那个字母上。

Such as:

如下:

bèi xià tiāo

③ Sometimes, the final is just composed of "i" and "u". The tone should be marked above the latter one.

韵母仅由 i 和 u 构成时,声调标在靠后的字母上。

Such as:

如下:

liú zuǐ huì

Tones are very important. Different tones show different meanings.

声调在汉语中很重要,不同的声调表示不同的意思。

Such as:

如下：

Syllables	Chinese Meanings	English Meanings
bā	八	eight
bá	拔	pull
bǎ	把	a quantifier
bà	爸	father

Some syllables do not have tones. Then the syllable has a neutral tone over the vowel. There is no tone mark.

有一些音节没有声调，这时，元音上的声调就是轻声，没有声调符号。

Such as:

如下：

Syllables	shénme	bùkèqi	xièxie
Chinese Meanings	什么	不客气	谢谢

The last syllable has no tone mark.

每个词的最后一个音节都没有声调标注。

1.1.4.1 Rules of Tone Changes

1.1.4.1.1 Third Tones

① If there are two syllables with third tones sitting side by side, then the tone of the former syllable is changed to a second tone.

当两个三声音节连在一起时，前面的三声音节改读成二声。

Such as:

如下：

"nǐhǎo"has two third tones, so it is changed to "níhǎo".

The same is true for"hěnhǎo" →"hénhǎo".

nǐhǎo 有两个三声，应该改读为 níhǎo。

hěnhǎo→hénhǎo 也是同样的道理。

② A third tone syllable should be read as a half third tone when it is followed by a first, second, fourth or neutral tone syllable.

三声音节后边跟一声、二声、四声或轻声音节时，应该读作半三声。

Such as:

如下：

(half third tone) ↓ yǔyī→yǔyī 雨衣→雨衣	(half third tone) ↓ hěnmáng→hěnmáng 很忙→很忙	(half third tone) ↓ wǔfàn→wǔfàn 午饭→午饭	(half third tone) ↓ hǎoma→hǎoma 好吗→好吗

③ When there are three third tones, generally, the two former third tones syllables turn into two second tones syllables and the third syllable is still the third tone or turns into the half third tone. If there is an emphasis on the first syllable or a pause behind the first syllable, the first syllable should turn into a half third tone syllable, the second syllable should turn into the second tone, and the third syllable keep the third tone.

三个三声音节在一起时，一般情况下，前两个三声音节变成二声音节，第三个音节保持第三声或者变成半三声。如果强调第一个三声音节或它后面有停顿时，则第一个三声音节要读半三声，第二个三声音节要读二声，第三个三声音节不变。

Such as:

如下：

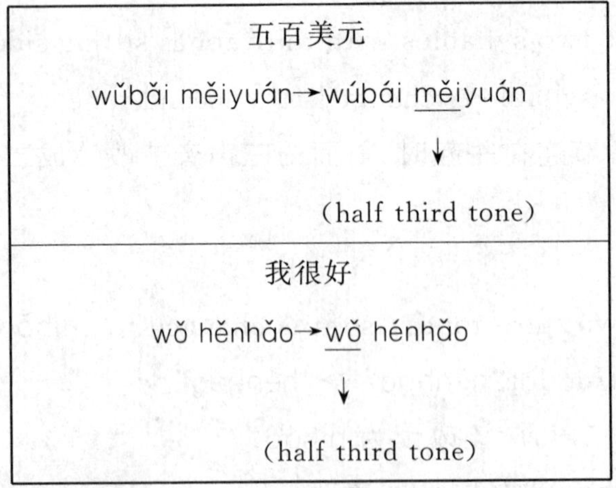

五百美元 wǔbǎi měiyuán→wúbái měiyuán ↓ (half third tone)
我很好 wǒ hěnhǎo→wǒ hénhǎo ↓ (half third tone)

1.1.4.1.2 Special Chinese Characters with Tone Changes

① The original tone for the Chinese Character "不" is the fourth tone. If there is another fourth tone syllable behind it, it turns into a second tone syllable.

"不"字的本调是四声。但当其后有一个四声音节时，它变为二声音节。

Such as:

如下：

bùhē 不喝	bùnán 不难	bùhǎo 不好	búqù 不去
bùgāo 不高	bùlái 不来	bùxiǎo 不小	búxiè 不谢

② The Chinese Character "一"。

Syllables	Examples	Note
yī	yī èr sān 一、二、三 dì yī 第 一 sān shí yī 三 十 一	When the character is an independent part to read or it is in the end of a word, it is a first tone syllable. 单念或在末尾时念一声。
yí	yí rì 一 日 yí wàn 一 万	If there is a fourth tone syllable behind it, it turns into a second tone syllable. 在四声音节前变为二声音节。
yì	yì nián 一 年 yì qǐ 一 起	If there is a first, second or third tone syllable behind it, it turns into a fourth tone syllable. 在一、二、三声音节前变为四声音节。
yi	shì yi shì 试 一 试 kàn yi kàn 看 一 看 xiǎng yi xiǎng 想 一 想	If it is between two same verbs, it turns into a neutral tone. 夹在重叠动词中间的时候，念轻声。

续表

Syllables	Examples	Note
yi	qù yi tàng 去 一 趟 guì yi xiē 贵 一 些 hǎo yi xiē 好 一 些	If it is among a verb, an adjective and a quantifier, it turns into a neutral tone. 用在动词、形容词与量词之间，念轻声。

1.1.5 Spelling Sorts of Pinyin

Syllables consist of entirety syllables, two-spelling syllables, three-spelling syllables and non-initial syllables.

音节包括整体认读音节、两拼音节、三拼音节和零声母音节。

Syllables
- Entirety Syllables
- Two-spelling Syllables
- Three-spelling Syllables
- Non-Initial Syllables

1.1.5.1 Entirety Syllables

It means we needn't to spell. There are 16 entirety syllables.

整体认读音节不需要拼读。整体认读音节一共有 16 个。

They are :

它们是：

zhi	chi	shi	ri	zi	ci	si	yi
wu	yu	ye	yue	yuan	yin	yun	ying

They can be divided into two categories.

它们可以分为两类。

① There are 7 entirety syllables which only pronounce initials. They are:

有 7 个整体认读音节，发音时只用发声母的音。它们是：

zhi=zh	chi=ch	shi=sh	ri=r	zi=z	ci=c	si=s

② There are nine entirety syllables which only pronounce finals. They are:

有九个整体认读音节，发音时只用发韵母的音。它们是：

yi=i	wu=u	yu=u=ü	ye=ie=yie	yue=ue=üe
yuan=uan=üan		yin=in	yun=un=ün	ying=ing

NOTE:

See NOTES in "Finals 1.1.3".

参照"韵母 1.1.3"中的注释。

1.1.5.2 Two-Spelling Syllables

It is composed of only one initial and one final. Such as:

只由一个声母和一个韵母组成的音节叫两拼音节。例如：

mì	fēng	zài	cǎi	mì
jīng	yú	zài	pēn	shuǐ
hóng	qí	gāo	shēng	qǐ

Here are some most used two-spelling syllables in Mandarin.

以下是普通话中常用的两拼音节。

B

bā bá bǎ bà ba

bāi bái bǎi bài bai

bān bǎn bàn

bāng bǎng bàng

bāo báo bǎo bào

bēi běi bèi bei

bēn běn bèn

bēng béng běng bèng

bī bí bǐ bì

biē bié biě biè

bīn bìn

bīng bǐng bìng

bō bó bǒ bò bo

bū bú bǔ bù

P

pā pá pà
pāi pái pǎi pài
pān pán pàn
pāng páng pǎng pàng
pāo páo pǎo pào
pēi péi pèi
pēn pén pèn
pēng péng pěng pèng
pī pí pǐ pì
piē piě piè
pīn pín pǐn pìn
pīng píng
pō pó pǒ pò po
pōu póu pǒu
pū pú pǔ pù

M

mā má mǎ mà ma
mái mǎi mài
mān mán mǎn màn
māng máng mǎng
māo máo mǎo mào
me
méi měi mèi
mēn mén mèn men
mēng méng měng mèng
mī mí mǐ mì
miē miè mín mǐn
míng mǐng mìng
miù
mō mó mǒ mò
mōu móu mǒu
mú mǔ mù

F

fā fá fǎ fà fa
fān fán fǎn fàn
fāng fáng fǎng fàng
fēi féi fěi fèi
fēn fén fěn fèn
fēng féng fěng fèng
fó
fǒu
fū fú fǔ fù

D

dā dá dǎ dà da
dāi dǎi dài
dān dǎn dàn
dāng dǎng dàng
dāo dáo dǎo dào
dē dé de
dēi děi
dèn
dēng děng dèng
dī dí dǐ dì
diē dié
dīng dǐng dìng
diū
dōng dǒng dòng

dōu dǒu dòu
dū dú dǔ dù
duī duì
dūn dǔn dùn

T

tā tǎ tà
tāi tái tǎi tài
tān tán tǎn tàn
tāng táng tǎng tàng
tāo táo tǎo tào
tè te
tēi
tēng téng
tī tí tǐ tì
tiē tiě tiè
tīng tíng tǐng tìng
tōng tóng tǒng tòng
tōu tóu tǒu tòu
tū tú tǔ tù
tuī tuí tuǐ tuì
tūn tún tǔn tùn

N

nā ná nǎ nà na
nǎi nài
nān nán nǎn nàn
nāng náng nǎng nàng
nāo náo nǎo nào
né nè ne
něi nèi
nèn
néng
nī ní nǐ nì
niē nié niè
nín
níng nǐng nìng
niū niú niǔ niù
nóng nòng
nòu
nú nǔ nù
nǚ nǜ
nüè

L

lā lá lǎ là la
lái lài lai
lán lǎn làn
lāng láng lǎng làng
lāo láo lǎo lào
lē lè le
lēi léi lěi lèi lei
lēng léng lěng lèng
lī lí lǐ lì li
liē liě liè lie
līn lín lǐn lìn
líng lǐng lìng
liū liú liǔ liù
lo
lōng lóng lǒng lòng
lōu lóu lǒu lòu lou
lū lú lǔ lù lu

lǘ lǚ lǜ

lüè

lūn lún lùn

G

gā gá gǎ gà

gāi gǎi gài

gān gǎn gàn

gāng gǎng gàng

gāo gǎo gào

gē gé gě gè

gěi

gēn gén gěn gèn

gēng gěng gèng

gōng gǒng gòng

gōu gǒu gòu

gū gǔ gù

guī guǐ guì

gǔn gùn

K

kā kǎ

kāi kǎi kài

kān kǎn kàn

kāng kǎng kàng

kāo kǎo kào

kē ké kě kè

kēi

kěn

kēng

kōng kǒng kòng

kōu kǒu kòu

kū kǔ kù

kuī kuí kuǐ kuì

kūn kǔn

H

hā há hǎ hà

hē hé hè

hū hú hǔ hù

hāi hái hǎi hài

hān hán hǎn hàn

hāng háng hàng

hāo hǎo hào

hēi

hén hěn hèn

hēng héng hèng

hōng hóng hǒng hòng

hōu hóu hǒu hòu

huī huí huǐ huì

hūn hún hùn

J

jī jí jǐ jì

jiē jié jiě jiè jie

jīn jǐn jìn

jīng jǐng jìng

jīu jǐu jìu jiu

jū jú jǔ jù

juē jué juě juè

jūn jùn

Q

qī qí qǐ qì

qiē qié qiě qiè

qīn qín qǐn qìn

qīng qíng qǐng qìng

qiū qiú qiǔ

qū qú qǔ qù qu

quē qué què

qūn qún

X

xī xí xǐ xì

xiē xié xiě xiè

xīn xín xǐn xìn

xīng xíng xǐng xìng

xiū xiǔ xiù

xū xú xǔ xù xu

xuē xué xuě xuè

xūn xún xùn

Zh

zhā zhá zhǎ zhà zha

zhāi zhái zhǎi zhài

zhān zhǎn zhàn

zhāng zhǎng zhàng

zhāo zháo zhǎo zhào

zhē zhé zhě zhè zhe

zhèi

zhēn zhěn zhèn

zhēng zhěng zhèng

zhī zhí zhǐ zhì

zhōng zhǒng zhòng

zhōu zhóu zhǒu zhòu

zhū zhú zhǔ zhù

zhuī zhuì

zhūn zhǔn

Ch

chā chá chǎ chà

chāi chái chǎi chài

chān chán chǎn chàn

chāng cháng chǎng chàng

chāo cháo chǎo chào

chē chě chè

chēn chén chěn chèn chen

chēng chéng chěng chèng

chī chí chǐ chì

chōng chóng chǒng chòng

chōu chóu chǒu chòu

chū chú chǔ chù

chuī chuí

chūn chún chǔn

Sh

shā shá shǎ shà

shāi shǎi shài

shān shǎn shàn

shāng shǎng shàng shang

shāo sháo shǎo shào

shē shé shě shè

shéi

shēn shén shěn shèn

shēng shén shěng shèng

shī shí shǐ shì shi

shōu shóu shǒu shòu

shū shú shǔ shù

shuí shuǐ shuì

shǔn shun

R

rán rǎn

rāng ráng rǎng ràng

ráo rǎo rào

rě rè

rén rěn rèn

rēng réng

rì

róng rǒng

róu ròu

rú rǔ rù

ruí ruǐ ruì

rún rùn

Z

zā zá zǎ

zāi zǎi zài

zán zǎn zàn zan

zāng zǎng zàng

zāo záo zǎo zào

zé zè

zéi

zěn zèn

zēng zèng

zī zǐ zì

zōng zǒng zòng

zōu zǒu zòu

zú zǔ

zuī zuǐ zuì

zūn zǔn zùn

C

cā cǎ

cāi cái cǎi cài

cān cán cǎn càn

cāng cáng

cāo cáo cǎo cào

cè

cèi

cēn cén

cēng céng cèng

cī cí cǐ cì

cōng cóng

còu

cū cú cù

cuī cuǐ cuì

cūn cún cǔn cùn

S

sā sǎ sà

sāi sài

sān sǎn sàn

sāng sǎng sàng

sāo sǎo sào

sè

sēn

sēng

sī sí sì

sōng sóng sǒng sòng

sōu sǒu sòu

sū sú sù

suī suí suǐ suì

sūn sǔn

Y

yā yá yǎ yà ya

yān yán yǎn yàn

yāng yáng yǎng yàng

yāo yáo yǎo yào

yē yé yě yè

yī yí yǐ yì

yīn yín yǐn yìn

yīng yíng yǐng yìng

yō yo

yōng yóng yǒng yòng

yōu yóu yǒu yòu

yū yú yǔ yù

yuē yué yuě yuè

yūn yún yǔn yùn

W

wā wá wǎ wà wa

wāi wǎi wài

wān wán wǎn wàn

wāng wáng wǎng wàng

wēi wéi wěi wèi

wēn wén wěn wèn

wēng wěng wèng

wō wǒ wò

wū wú wǔ wù

1.1.5.3 Three-Spelling Syllables

It is composed of one initial and two finals. The first final is a transition and connects the initial and the second final. Such as:

三拼音节由一个声母和两个韵母组成。其中，第一个韵母起过渡作用，连接声母和第二个韵母。例如：

xiǎo	piào	liàng	xiàng	guǎi	shuāi

Here are some most used three-spelling syllables in Mandarin.

以下是普通话中常用的三拼音节。

B

biān biǎn biàn

biāo biǎo biào

P

piān piàn piǎn piàn

piāo piáo piǎo piào

M

miān miǎn miàn

miāo miáo miǎo miào

D

diǎ

diān diǎn diàn

diāo diǎo diào

duān duǎn duàn

duō duó duǒ duò

T

tiān tián tiǎn tiàn

tiāo tiáo tiǎo tiào

tuān tuán tuǎn tuàn

tuō tuó tuǒ tuò

N

niān nián niǎn niàn

niáng niàng

niǎo niào

nuǎn

nuó nuò

L

liǎ

lián liǎn liàn

liáng liǎng liàng

liāo liáo liǎo liào

luán luǎn luàn

luō luó luǒ luò luo

G

guā guǎ guà

guāi guǎi guài

guān guǎn guàn

guāng guǎng guàng

guō guó guǒ guò

K

kuā kuǎ kuà

kuǎi kuài

kuān kuǎn

kuāng kuáng kuǎng kuàng

kuò

H

huā huá huà

huái huài huai

huān huán huǎn huàn

huāng huáng huǎng huàng

huō huó huǒ huò

J

jiā jiá jiǎ jià

jiān jiǎn jiàn

jiāng jiǎng jiàng

jiāo jiáo jiǎo jiào

juān juǎn juàn

Q

qiā qiá qiǎ qià

qiān qián qiǎn qiàn

qiāng qiáng qiǎng qiàng

qiāo qiáo qiǎo qiào

qióng

quān quán quǎn quàn

X

xiā xiá xià

xiān xián xiǎn xiàn

xiāng xiáng xiǎng xiàng

xiāo xiáo xiǎo xiào

xiōng xióng xiòng

Zh

zhuā zhuǎ

zhuāi zhuǎi zhuài

zhuān zhuǎn zhuàn

zhuāng zhuǎng zhuàng

zhuō zhuó

Ch

chuā

chuāi chuái chuǎi chuài

chuān chuán chuǎn chuàn

chuāng chuáng chuǎng

chuàng

chuō chuò

Sh

shuā shuǎ shuà

shuāi shuǎi shuài

shuān shuàn

shuāng shuǎng

shuō shuò

R

ruá

ruán ruǎn

ruó ruò

Z

zuān zuǎn zuàn

zuō zuó zuǒ zuò

C

cuān cuán cuàn

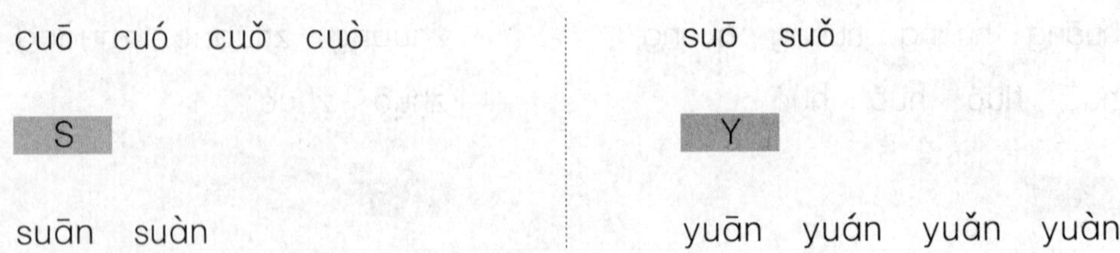

1.1.5.4 Non-Initial Syllables

It is composed of only one final. Such as:
只有一个韵母的音节叫作零声母音节。例如：

ā á ǎ à a	ō ó ǒ ò	ē é ě è e

Here are some most used no initial syllables in Mandarin:
以下是普通话中常用的零声母音节：

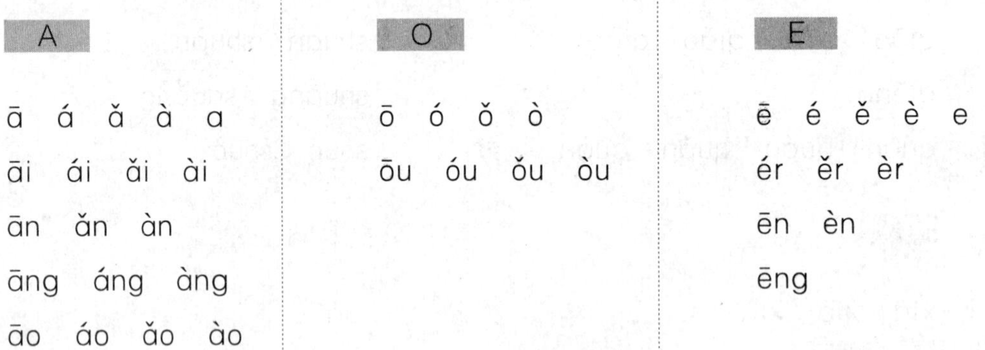

1.1.6 Dividing Marks

When a syllable beginning or ending with "ɑ, o, e" connects with another syllable, a dividing mark (') should be added to clarify the boundary between the two syllables.

以 ɑ、o、e 开头或结尾的音节连接其他音节时，应该用一个分隔符号(')来澄清两个音节之间的界限。

Such as:

如下：

dáàn(答案)	mùǒu(木偶)	ēnài(恩爱)	míngé(名额)
↓	↓	↓	↓
dá'àn(答案)	mù'ǒu(木偶)	ēn'ài(恩爱)	míng'é(名额)

1.1.7 Er and Retroflex Syllables

Chinese character "儿" pronounces "ér". "er"forms a retroflex syllable in combination with other finals. When writing a retroflex syllable, you should add a " r " after the original final. When writing a Chinese character, you should add" 儿 " after the original character. Sometimes you can chose not to add.

"儿"字发 ér 音。er 与其他韵母结合成儿化韵母。儿化韵母的写法是在原韵母之后加 r。汉字写法是在原汉字之后写个"儿"字,有时可省略不写。

Such as:

如下：

huà 画	nǎ 哪	wán 玩
↓	↓	↓
huàr 画儿	nǎr 哪儿	wánr 玩儿

How to pronounce "er ": first put the tongue in the position for " e ", then slightly curl up the tongue-tip, trying to pronounce the " er ".

如何发 er 音:先把舌头放到发 e 的位置,然后将舌尖轻轻上翘,同时发 er 的音。

1.1.8 Summary

Initials

b p m f
d t n l
g k h
j q x
zh ch sh r
z c s
y w

Frequently Used Finals

a	o	e	i	u	ü			
ai	ei	ui	ao	ou	iu	ie	üe	er
an	en	in	un	ün	ang	eng	ing	ong

All Finals

	i	u	ü
a	ia	ua	
o		uo	
e	ie		üe
ai		uai	
ei		ui	
ao	iao		
ou	iu		
an	ian	uan	üan
en	in	un	ün
ang	iang	uang	
eng	ing	ueng	
ong	iong		

NOTE:

Besides all above, "er" is also a final.

Single Finals & Compound Finals

<table>
<tr><th>Category</th><th>Letters</th><th colspan="6">Finals</th><th colspan="3">Quantity</th></tr>
<tr><td>single</td><td>1</td><td>a</td><td>o</td><td>e</td><td>i</td><td>u</td><td>ü</td><td colspan="3">6</td></tr>
<tr><td rowspan="5">compound</td><td rowspan="4">2</td><td colspan="2">ai</td><td colspan="2">ei</td><td colspan="2">ui</td><td colspan="2" rowspan="3">9</td><td rowspan="5">18</td></tr>
<tr><td colspan="2">ao</td><td colspan="2">ou</td><td colspan="2">iu</td></tr>
<tr><td colspan="2">ie</td><td colspan="2">üe</td><td colspan="2">er</td></tr>
<tr><td>an</td><td>en</td><td>in</td><td>un</td><td>ün</td><td></td><td>5</td><td rowspan="2">9</td></tr>
<tr><td>3</td><td>ang</td><td>eng</td><td>ing</td><td>ong</td><td></td><td></td><td>4</td></tr>
</table>

Compound Finals

Category	Finals					Quantity
lateral	ai		ei		ui	9
	ao		ou		iu	
	ie		üe		er	
nasal	an	en	in	un	ün	9
	ang	eng	ing	ong		

Nasal Sound

Category	Nasal Sound					Quantity
front	an	en	in	un	ün	5
back	ang	eng	ing	ong		4

1.2 Pronunciation Exercises

There is no real religion in China. All the existing religions were introduced from abroad. Some people say that Taoism is a local religion in China. It's not really. Because Taoism does not have any god, it only explores the relationship between human and nature, and speculates if there is a god or not. The current popular religions in China are Buddhism (most Chinese believe it more or less); Islam (in some areas, we call it The Muslim); Christianity; Catholicism, etc.

What do the Chinese people believe in? The popular saying is that the Chinese believe in Confucianism. The ancient sage, great thinker, philosopher and educator: Confucius, who created a set of thought theories that evolved into codes of conduct and were observed and practiced by the Chinese people, and slowly implanted into thousands of years of the Chinese history, culture, society and people's heart.

Dizigui and *Sanzijing* are very famous literature in the Chinese history. It is written according to the thoughts in Confucius' analects. As a result of its catchy pronunciation and simple meaning, *Dizigui* and *Sanzijing* have been handed down for many years, and are still used in schools as classics of Chinese studies to be repeatedly recited and studied.

Many of the ideas in *Dizigui* and *Sanzijing* are similar to those in the Bible or Koran, such as the ten commandments of Moses, which require people to honor their parents and love others as themselves. Their rules contain detailed instructions and codes of conduct on how to honor one's parents. Although these rules are outdated in modern society, but the Chinese in ancient times strictly followed them. They also taught in detail how to love your neighbor as yourself, as the Bible says: "If you love only those who love you, what reward is there for you? Even sinners love those who love them."

China's Confucianism has much in common with some largest religions of the world. There are many things in traditional Chinese culture and customs that are similar to those in other religions, which are worth studying and researching.

1.2.1 *Dizigui*

1.2.1.1 Introduction

Dizigui was written by Li Yuxiu in the Qing Dynasty during the reign of the Kangxi Emperor (1661—1722). The book is based on ancient teachings of the Chinese philosopher Confucius and emphasizes the basic rules for being a good person and the guidelines for living in peace with others. Like *Sanzijing* (another classic Chinese children's text), it is written in three-character verses.

Confucius emphasized that we should teach a young kid the basic moral values and manners first. Those values are to respect elders, respect brothers and sisters, respect one's wife or husband, respect the society and the whole country. He believed that all other learning would turn to nothing without those values. The teachings in *Dizigui* have been standard teachings for the young in China for thousand years.

《弟子规》是李毓秀在清朝康熙皇帝(1661—1722)统治期间所著。该书以中国哲学家孔子的教诲为基础,强调成为贤者的基本要求和与他人和睦相处的重要规则。和《三字经》(另一部中国儿童经典文本)一样,《弟子规》用三字诗的形式编写成。

孔子强调,从小就应该先教给孩子基本的道德价值观和美德。比如尊重长辈,尊重兄弟姐妹,尊重妻子和丈夫,尊重社会,以及尊重整个国家。他相信,如果没有这些价值观的学习,其他学习将无济于事。几千年来,《弟子规》一直是中国年轻人的行为标准。

1.2.1.2 Passage

zǒng xù
总 叙

Preface

dì zǐ guī shèng rén xùn
弟子规，圣人训。

Standards for being a good student and child are teachings from the ancient Chinese saints and sages.

shǒu xiào tì cì jǐn xìn
首孝悌，次谨信。

First，you should be dutiful to your parents and love and respect your siblings. Then you should be cautious about your daily words and behavior，and be a trusty person.

fàn ài zhòng ér qīn rén
泛爱众，而亲仁。

Furthermore，you should love all equally，and be close to the people of virtue，and learn from them.

yǒu yú lì zé xué wén
有余力，则学文。

Having accomplished all above，you can go further to study literature，art and other beneficial subjects.

dì yī zhāng rù zé xiào
第一章 入则孝

Chapter 1 At Home，Be Dutiful to Parents

dì yī jié
第一节

Section 1

fù mǔ hū yìng wù huǎn
父母呼，应勿缓。

When your parents call you，answer them right away.

fù mǔ mìng xíng wù lǎn
父母命，行勿懒。

When they tell you to do something，do it quickly.

fù mǔ jiào xū jìng tīng 父母教，须敬听。	When your parents instruct you, listen respectfully.
fù mǔ zé xū shùn chéng 父母责，须顺承。	When they reproach you, obey and accept it.
dì èr jié **第二节**	**Section 2**
dōng zé wēn xià zé qìng 冬则温，夏则凊。	In winter, keep your parents warm. In summer, keep them cool.
chén zé xǐng hūn zé dìng 晨则省，昏则定。	Visit and greet your parents in the morning to care them. Visit and greet your parents at dusk to make sure they rest well.
chū bì gào fǎn bì miàn 出必告，反必面。	Before going out, tell your parents where you are going, because they are always concerned about you. After returning, visit them and let them know you are back, so they do not worry about you.
jū yǒu cháng yè wú biàn 居有常，业无变。	Hold on your dreams and careers. Do not change them casually.
dì sān jié **第三节**	**Section 3**
shì suī xiǎo wù shàn wéi 事虽小，勿擅为。	Even it is a tiny matter, you should not decide on your own casually.
gǒu shàn wéi zǐ dào kuī 苟擅为，子道亏。	If so, you are against the standards.
wù suī xiǎo wù sī cáng 物虽小，勿私藏。	Even it is a small asset, you should not keep it from your parents.

gǒu sī cáng qīn xīn shāng
苟私藏，亲心伤。

Otherwise, your parents will be upset.

dì sì jié 第四节

Section 4

qīn suǒ hào lì wèi jù
亲所好，力为具。

Whatever pleases your parents, try your best to get it for them.

qīn suǒ wù jǐn wèi qù
亲所恶，谨为去。

Whatever annoys them, you should cautiously keep it away from them.

shēn yǒu shāng yí qīn yōu
身有伤，贻亲忧。

When your body is hurt, your parents will be worried.

dé yǒu shāng yí qīn xiū
德有伤，贻亲羞。

If your behavior is immoral, your parents will feel ashamed.

dì wǔ jié 第五节

Section 5

qīn ài wǒ xiào hé nán
亲爱我，孝何难。

When your parents love and please you, it is easy to be a dutiful child.

qīn zēng wǒ xiào fāng xián
亲憎我，孝方贤。

When your parents rebuke and annoy you, it is virtuous if you are still dutiful to them.

dì liù jié 第六节

Section 6

qīn yǒu guò jiàn shǐ gēng
亲有过，谏使更。

When your parents do something wrong, persuade them to correct it.

yí wú sè róu wú shēng
怡吾色，柔吾声。

Act with kind facial expressions and a gentle tone when you suggest.

jiàn bù rù yuè fù jiàn
谏不入，悦复谏。

If they do not accept, persuade them again when they are in a happier mood.

háo qì suí tà wú yuàn
号泣随，挞无怨。

Or using tears to move them, if being punished, you should never complain.

dì qī jié
第七节

Section 7

qīn yǒu jí yào xiān cháng
亲有疾，药先尝。

When your parents fall ill, taste the decoction before they take it.
(To tell whether it is too hot or bitter)

zhòu yè shì bù lí chuáng
昼夜侍，不离床。

Take care of your parents day and night. Do not be far from their bedsides.

sāng sān nián cháng bēi yè
丧三年，常悲咽。

During the first 3 years after your parents passed away, you should always recall and be grateful to them.

jū chù biàn jiǔ ròu jué
居处变，酒肉绝。

You should make some changes to reflect your grief and sorrow in your daily life. You cannot eat meat or have alcohol.

dì bā jié
第八节

Section 8

sāng jìn lǐ jì jìn chéng
丧尽礼，祭尽诚。

Obey the manners strictly at the funeral. The sacrifice ceremony must show your sincerity.

shì sǐ zhě rú shì shēng
事死者，如事生。

Serve your departed parents as if they were still alive.

dì èr zhāng chū zé tì
第二章 出则悌

Chapter 2 Standards for Adults in Society

dì yī jié
第一节

Section 1

xiōng dào yǒu dì dào gōng
兄道友，弟道恭。

The older siblings should befriend the younger ones, and the younger siblings should respect the older ones.

xiōng dì mù xiào zài zhōng
兄弟睦，孝在中。

The harmonious relationship between the siblings are actually dutiful to their parents.

cái wù qīng yuàn hé shēng
财物轻，怨何生。

If you are not mean with belongings, there will be no resentment in your family.

yán yǔ rěn fèn zì mǐn
言语忍，忿自泯。

If you are careful with words, there will be no annoyance in your family.

dì èr jié
第二节

Section 2

huò yǐn shí huò zuò zǒu
或饮食，或坐走。

Whether you are drinking, eating, walking, or sitting,

zhǎng zhě xiān yòu zhě hòu
长者先，幼者后。

let elders go first, then the younger ones.

zhǎng hū rén jí dài jiào
长呼人，即代叫。

When an elder is calling someone, you should get the person for him right away.

rén bù zài jǐ jí dào
人不在，己即到。

If you cannot find that person, you should ask the elder what you can do for him.

dì sān jié
第三节

Section 3

chēng zūn zhǎng wù hū míng
称尊长，勿呼名。

When you address an elder, do not call the given name.

duì zūn zhǎng wù xiàn néng
对尊长，勿见能。

In front of an elder, do not show off your talent.

lù yù zhǎng jí qū yī
路遇长，疾趋揖。

When meeting an elder on the street, you should greet and make a bow with hands folded in front quickly.

zhǎng wú yán, tuì gōng lì
长无言，退恭立。

If the elder does not respond, you should step back and stand aside respectfully.

dì sì jié
第四节

Section 4

qí xià mǎ, chéng xià chē
骑下马，乘下车。

When meeting an elder on the street, you would get down to greet the elder whether riding on a horse or sitting in a carriage.

guò yóu dài, bǎi bù yú
过犹待，百步余。

When he is passing by, you should stand aside and wait respectfully. Do not leave until he is about 100 steps from you.

dì wǔ jié
第五节

Section 5

zhǎng zhě lì, yòu wù zuò
长者立，幼勿坐。

When an elder is standing, the younger ones cannot sit down.

zhǎng zhě zuò, mìng nǎi zuò
长者坐，命乃坐。

After the elder sits down, you can sit down only when you are told.

zūn zhǎng qián, shēng yào dī
尊长前，声要低。

In front of an elder, speak clearly and softly.

dī bù wén, què fēi yí
低不闻，却非宜。

If your voice is too low to hear, that is not good.

dì liù jié
第六节

Section 6

jìn bì qū, tuì bì chí
进必趋，退必迟。

When you meet an elder, you should walk quickly to him. When leaving, you should exit slowly.

wèn qǐ duì shì wù yí
问起对,视勿移。

When an elder ask you, you should stand up to reply, and do not move your sight away.

dì qī jié
第七节

Section 7

shì zhū fù rú shì fù
事诸父,如事父。

When serving your uncles, do as you do to your father.

shì zhū xiōng rú shì xiōng
事诸兄,如事兄。

When getting on with your cousins, do as if they are your own siblings.

dì sān zhāng jǐn
第三章 谨

Chapter 3 Be Cautious in Your Daily Life

dì yī jié
第一节

Section 1

zhāo qǐ zǎo yè mián chí
朝起早,夜眠迟。

Get up early in the morning, and do not go to bed early at night.

lǎo yì zhì xī cǐ shí
老易至,惜此时。

Time is passing by quickly,
you should treasure the present.

chén bì guàn jiān shù kǒu
晨必盥,兼漱口。

When getting up in the morning,
wash your face and brush your teeth.

biàn niào huí zhé jìng shǒu
便溺回,辄净手。

After using the toilet,
always wash your hands.

dì èr jié
第二节

Section 2

guān bì zhèng niǔ bì jié
冠必正,纽必结。

You must wear your hat rightly, and make sure the buttons of your clothes are tied.

wà yǔ lǚ jù jǐn qiè
袜与履，俱紧切。
Make sure your socks and shoes are neatly and correctly worn.

zhì guān fú yǒu dìng wèi
置冠服，有定位。
Place your hat and clothes in their proper places.

wù luàn dùn zhì wū huì
勿乱顿，致污秽。
Do not carelessly throw your clothes around, otherwise they will get dirty.

dì sān jié
第三节 Section 3

yī guì jié bù guì huá
衣贵洁，不贵华。
It is more important that your clothes are clean rather than how gorgeous they are.

shàng xún fèn xià chèn jiā
上循分，下称家。
Your clothes should be suitable for your social station and your family condition.

duì yǐn shí wù jiǎn zé
对饮食，勿拣择。
When it comes to diet, you should avoid being a picky eater.

shí shì kě wù guò zé
食适可，勿过则。
Eating the right amount, do not over-eat.

dì sì jié
第四节 Section 4

nián fāng shào wù yǐn jiǔ
年方少，勿饮酒。
You are still young, and do not drink alcohol.

yǐn jiǔ zuì zuì wéi chǒu
饮酒醉，最为丑。
When you are drunk, your behavior will turn ugly.

bù cóng róng lì duān zhèng
步从容，立端正。
Walk unhurriedly, and stand up straight.

yī shēn yuán bài gōng jìng
揖深圆，拜恭敬。

When greeting others, you should make a deep bow with hands folded in front respectfully.

wù jiàn yù wù bǒ yǐ
勿践阈，勿跛倚。

Do not step on doorsills when coming in. Do not stand leaning on one leg.

wù jī jù wù yáo bì
勿箕踞，勿摇髀。

Do not sit with your legs stretched out. Do not shake your legs.

dì wǔ jié
第五节

Section 5

huǎn jiē lián wù yǒu shēng
缓揭帘，勿有声。

Lift the curtain slowly. Do not make any noise.

kuān zhuǎn wān wù chù léng
宽转弯，勿触棱。

Leave yourself some room when you turn and make sure you do not bump into a corner.

zhí xū qì rú zhí yíng
执虚器，如执盈。

Hold empty containers carefully as if they were full.

rù xū shì rú yǒu rén
入虚室，如有人。

Enter empty rooms as if they were occupied.

dì liù jié
第六节

Section 6

shì wù máng máng duō cuò
事勿忙，忙多错。

Avoid doing things in a hurry. Otherwise, you will make many mistakes.

wù wèi nán wù qīng lüè
勿畏难，勿轻略。

Do not be afraid of difficult tasks. Do not become careless when a job is so easy.

dòu nào chǎng jué wù jìn
斗闹场，绝勿近。

Keep away from rowdy places.

xié pì shì jué wù wèn
邪僻事，绝勿问。

Do not ask about abnormal or indecent things.

dì qī jié 第七节 Section 7

jiāng rù mén wèn shú cún
将入门，问孰存。

When you are to enter a door, ask if anyone is inside.

jiāng shàng táng shēng bì yáng
将上堂，声必扬。

Before entering the living room, make yourself heard so that those inside know someone is approaching.

rén wèn shuí duì yǐ míng
人问谁，对以名。

If someone asks who you are, you should give your name.

wú yǔ wǒ bù fēn míng
吾与我，不分明。

To answer with "It is me" or "Me" is unidentified.

dì bā jié 第八节 Section 8

yòng rén wù xū míng qiú
用人物，须明求。

Before borrowing things from others, you must ask for permission.

tǎng bù wèn jí wéi tōu
倘不问，即为偷。

If you do not ask, you are stealing.

jiè rén wù jí shí huán
借人物，及时还。

After borrowing things from others, you should return them on time.

hòu yǒu jí jiè bù nán
后有急，借不难。

Later, when you have an urgent need, it is not difficult to borrow again.

dì sì zhāng xìn
第四章 信

Chapter 4 Be Trustworthy

dì yī jié
第一节

Section 1

fán chū yán, xìn wéi xiān
凡出言,信为先。

When you speak, honesty is important.

zhà yǔ wàng, xī kě yān
诈与妄,奚可焉。

Deceitful words and lies are not allowed.

huà shuō duō, bù rú shǎo
话说多,不如少。

Rather than talking too much, it is better to speak less.

wéi qí shì, wù nìng qiǎo
惟其是,勿佞巧。

Speak the truth, and do not twist the facts.

jiān qiǎo yǔ, huì wū cí
奸巧语,秽污词。

Cunning words, foul language

shì jǐng qì, qiè jiè zhī
市井气,切戒之。

and bad habits must be avoided at all costs.

dì èr jié
第二节

Section 2

jiàn wèi zhēn, wù qīng yán
见未真,勿轻言。

What you have not seen with your own eyes, you should not readily tell to others.

zhī wèi dì, wù qīng chuán
知未的,勿轻传。

What you do not know for sure, you should not easily pass on to others.

shì fēi yí, wù qīng nuò
事非宜,勿轻诺。

When asked to do something that is inappropriate or bad, you should not promise lightly.

gǒu qīng nuò, jìn tuì cuò
苟轻诺,进退错。

If you do, you will be wrong either way.

dì sān jié 第三节 Section 3

fán dào zì zhòng qiě shū
凡道字，重且舒。

When speaking, make the words clear and to the point.

wù jí jí wù mó hu
勿急疾，勿模糊。

Do not talk too fast or mumble.

bǐ shuō cháng cǐ shuō duǎn
彼说长，此说短。

Some like to talk about the good points of others, while some like to talk about the faults of others.

bù guān jǐ mò xián guǎn
不关己，莫闲管。

If it is none of your business, you should not get involved.

dì sì jié 第四节 Section 4

jiàn rén shàn jí sī qí
见人善，即思齐。

When you see others do good deeds, think about following their examples.

zòng qù yuǎn yǐ jiàn jī
纵去远，以渐跻。

Even though you are still far behind, you are getting closer.

jiàn rén è jí nèi xǐng
见人恶，即内省。

When you see others do wrong, immediately reflect upon yourself.

yǒu zé gǎi wú jiā jǐng
有则改，无加警。

If you have made the same mistake, correct it. If not, be extra cautious not to make the same mistake.

dì wǔ jié 第五节 Section 5

wéi dé xué wéi cái yì
唯德学，唯才艺。

You should pay more attention to your morals, conduct, knowledge, and skills.

bù rú rén dāng zì lì
不如人，当自砺。

If they are not as good as others', you should encourage yourself to be better.

ruò yī fú ruò yǐn shí
若衣服，若饮食。

Like the clothes you wear, and the food you eat and drink,

bù rú rén wù shēng qī
不如人，勿生戚。

if they are not as good as others', you should not be ashamed.

dì liù jié
第六节 Section 6

wén guò nù wén yù lè
闻过怒，闻誉乐。

If criticism makes you angry and compliments make you happy,

sǔn yǒu lái yì yǒu què
损友来，益友却。

bad company will come your way and good friends will shy away.

wén yù kǒng wén guò xīn
闻誉恐，闻过欣。

If you are uneasy about compliments and appreciative of criticism,

zhí liàng shì jiàn xiāng qīn
直谅士，渐相亲。

understanding and virtuous people will gradually be close to you.

dì qī jié
第七节 Section 7

wú xīn fēi míng wéi cuò
无心非，名为错。

If your error is not done on purpose, it is only a mistake.

yǒu xīn fēi míng wéi è
有心非，名为恶。

If it is done on purpose, it is evil.

guò néng gǎi guī yú wú
过能改，归于无。

If you correct your mistake and do not repeat it, the mistake made can be dispelled from the mind.

tǎng yǎn shì zēng yī gū
倘掩饰，增一辜。

If you try to cover it up, you will be doubly wrong.

dì wǔ zhāng fàn ài zhòng
第五章 泛爱众

Chapter 5 Love All Equally

dì yī jié
第一节

Section 1

fán shì rén jiē xū ài
凡是人，皆须爱。

Human beings, regardless of nationality, race, or religion, should be loved equally.

tiān tóng fù dì tóng zài
天同覆，地同载。

We are all sheltered by the same sky and live on the same planet Earth.

xìng gāo zhě míng zì gāo
行高者，名自高。

A person with high ideals and morals is highly respected.

rén suǒ zhòng fēi mào gāo
人所重，非貌高。

What people value is not based on outside appearance.

cái dà zhě wàng zì dà
才大者，望自大。

A person with outstanding ability will naturally have a good reputation.

rén suǒ fú fēi yán dà
人所服，非言大。

Admiration from others does not come from talking big or praising oneself.

dì èr jié
第二节

Section 2

jǐ yǒu néng wù zì sī
己有能，勿自私。

If you are a very capable person, use your capabilities for the benefit of others.

rén yǒu néng wù qīng zǐ
人有能，勿轻訾。

Other people's competence should not be slandered.

wù chǎn fù wù jiāo pín
勿谄富，勿骄贫。

Do not flatter the rich or despise the poor.

wù yàn gù wù xǐ xīn
勿厌故，勿喜新。

Do not ignore old friends, and take delight in new ones.

dì sān jié 第三节 Section 3

rén bù xián wù shì jiǎo
人不闲，勿事搅。

When a person is busy, do not bother him with matters.

rén bù ān wù huà rǎo
人不安，勿话扰。

When a person's mind is not at peace, do not bother him with words.

rén yǒu duǎn qiè mò jiē
人有短，切莫揭。

If a person has shortcomings, do not expose it.

rén yǒu sī qiè mò shuō
人有私，切莫说。

If a person has a secret, do not tell others.

dào rén shàn jí shì shàn
道人善，即是善。

Praising the goodness of others is a good deed in itself.

rén zhī zhī yù sī miǎn
人知之，愈思勉。

When people are approved and praised, they would feel encouraged and try even harder.

dì sì jié 第四节 Section 4

yáng rén è jí shì è
扬人恶，即是恶。

Spreading rumors about the wrongdoings of others is a wrongdoing in itself.

jí zhī shèn huò qiě zuò
疾之甚，祸且作。

If you blame and criticize others too much, you will also bring disaster to yourself.

shàn xiāng quàn dé jiē jiàn
善相劝，德皆建。

When encouraging others to do good, the virtues of both of yours are built up.

guò bù guī dào liǎng kuī
过不规，道两亏。

If you do not tell others of their faults, you will both be wrong.

dì wǔ jié 第五节 Section 5

fán qǔ yǔ guì fēn xiǎo
凡取与，贵分晓。

Whether you take or give, you need to know the difference between the two.

yǔ yí duō qǔ yí shǎo
与宜多，取宜少。

It is better to give more and take less.

jiāng jiā rén xiān wèn jǐ
将加人，先问己。

What you ask others to do, ask yourself first if you will do it.

jǐ bù yù jí sù yǐ
己不欲，即速已。

If it is not something you will do, do not ask others to do it.

ēn yù bào yuàn yù wàng
恩欲报，怨欲忘。

You must repay the kindness of others and let go of your resentments.

bào yuàn duǎn bào ēn cháng
抱怨短，报恩长。

Spend less time holding grudges and more time paying back the kindness of others.

dì liù jié 第六节 Section 6

dài bì pú shēn guì duān
待婢仆，身贵端。

When you are directing maids and servants, you should be respectable and dignified.

suī guì duān cí ér kuān
虽贵端，慈而宽。

Even though you are respectable and dignified, treat them kindly and generously.

shì fú rén xīn bù rán
势服人，心不然。

If you use your influence to make them submissive, their hearts will not be with you.

lǐ fú rén fāng wú yán
理服人，方无言。

If you can convince them with sound reasoning, they will have nothing more to say.

dì liù zhāng qīn rén
第六章 亲仁

Chapter 6 Be Close to and Learn from People of Virtue and Compassion

dì yī jié
第一节

Section 1

tóng shì rén lèi bù qí
同是人，类不齐。

We are all humans, but we are not the same.

liú sú zhòng rén zhě xī
流俗众，仁者稀。

Most of us are ordinary; only a very few have great virtues and high moral principles.

guǒ rén zhě rén duō wèi
果仁者，人多畏。

A truly virtuous person is greatly respected by others.

yán bù huì sè bù mèi
言不讳，色不媚。

He will not be afraid to speak the truth and will not fawn on others.

dì èr jié
第二节

Section 2

néng qīn rén wú xiàn hǎo
能亲仁，无限好。

If you are close to and learn from people of virtue and compassion, you will benefit immensely.

dé rì jìn guò rì shǎo 德日进，过日少。	Your virtues will grow daily, and your faults will lessen day by day.
bù qīn rén wú xiàn hài 不亲仁，无限害。	If you are not close to and learn from people of virtue and compassion, you will suffer a great loss.
xiǎo rén jìn bǎi shì huài 小人进，百事坏。	People without virtue will get close to you and nothing you do will succeed.

dì qī zhāng yú lì xué wén
第七章 余力学文

Chapter 7 After All the above Are Accomplished, Further Study and Learn Literature and Arts to Improve Your Cultural and Spiritual Life

dì yī jié
第一节

Section 1

bù lì xíng dàn xué wén 不力行，但学文。	If you do not actively make use of what you have learned, but continue to study on the surface,
zhǎng fú huá chéng hé rén 长浮华，成何人。	your knowledge is increasing, but it is only superficial. What kind of a person will you be?
dàn lì xíng bù xué wén 但力行，不学文。	If you do apply your knowledge diligently, but stop studying,
rèn jǐ jiàn mèi lǐ zhēn 任己见，昧理真。	you will stick to your opinion, without thinking whether it is correct; hence you are uninformed.

dì èr jié
第 二 节

Section 2

dú shū fǎ yǒu sān dào
读书法,有三到。

There are ways to study. They involve concentration in three areas.

xīn yǎn kǒu xìn jiē yào
心眼口,信皆要。

Your mind, your eyes, and your mouth are really important.

fāng dú cǐ wù mù bǐ
方读此,勿慕彼。

When you begin to read a book, do not think about another.

cǐ wèi zhōng bǐ wù qǐ
此未终,彼勿起。

If you have not completed the book, do not start another.

dì sān jié
第 三 节

Section 3

kuān wéi xiàn jǐn yòng gōng
宽为限,紧用功。

Give yourself lots of time to study, and study hard.

gōng fū dào zhì sè tōng
工夫到,滞塞通。

Given time and effort, you will thoroughly understand.

xīn yǒu yí suí zhá jì
心有疑,随札记。

If you have a question, make a note of it,

jiù rén wèn qiú què yì
就人问,求确义。

and ask the person who has the knowledge for the right answer.

dì sì jié
第 四 节

Section 4

fáng shì qīng qiáng bì jìng
房室清,墙壁净。

Keep your room neat, walls uncluttered and clean,

jī àn jié bǐ yàn zhèng 几案洁，笔砚正。	your desk tidy and your brushes and ink-stone properly placed.
mò mó piān xīn bù duān 墨磨偏，心不端。	If your ink block is ground unevenly, it shows you have a poor state of mind.
zì bù jìng xīn xiān bìng 字不敬，心先病。	When words are written carelessly, it shows your state of mind has not been well.

dì wǔ jié
第五节 Section 5

liè diǎn jí yǒu dìng chù 列典籍，有定处。	The books should be classified, placed on the bookshelves, in their proper places.
dú kàn bì huán yuán chù 读看毕，还原处。	After you finish reading a book, you should put it back in its right place.
suī yǒu jí juàn shù qí 虽有急，卷束齐。	Even though you are in a hurry, you should neatly put away the book you were reading.
yǒu quē huài jiù bǔ zhī 有缺坏，就补之。	Any missing or damaged pages ought to be repaired.

dì liù jié
第六节 Section 6

fēi shèng shū bǐng wù shì 非圣书，屏勿视。	If it is not a book on the teachings of saints and sages, you should not read it.
bì cōng míng huài xīn zhì 敝聪明，坏心志。	These books can block your intelligence and wisdom and will undermine your aspirations and sense of direction.

wù zì bào wù zì qì
勿 自 暴，勿 自 弃。

Neither resign yourself to failure.

shèng yǔ xián kě xún zhì
圣 与 贤，可 驯 致。

To be a person of high ideals, and virtue is something we can all attain in time.

1.2.2 *Sanzijing*

1.2.2.1 Introduction

The *Three-Character Classic*, also called the *Trimetric Classic* or *Sanzijing*, is one of the Chinese classic texts. It was probably written in the 13th century and mainly attributed to Wang Yinglin (王应麟，1223-1296) and Ou Shizi (区适子，1234-1324) in the Song dynasty, and was supplemented by others in the follow-up dynasties. It is not one of the traditional six Confucian classics, but good for teaching young children with Confucianism. Until the late part of the 1800s, it was used as a formal elementary education for children at home.

The text is written in three-word phrases for easy memorization. Because most people were not well-educated, dictation made it popular and preserved through centuries. With the help of simple texts in the *Three-Character Classic*, children learned many characters, grammar structures, Chinese history and Confucian morality, especially filial piety and respect for elders.

《三字经》被认为是中国文学经典。该书大约于 13 世纪由宋朝王应麟(1223—1296)与区适子(1234—1324)合著(存疑)，后世多有补充。这部著作不是传统的六经之一，而是适合幼儿教学的儒家思想的体现。直到 19 世纪后期，它才成为家中孩子启蒙的正规教育。

为了便于记忆，《三字经》全文用三字短句写成。当时大多数人文化水平都不高，口述传统确保了它在几百年中流行和存续。通过诵读三字诗句，孩子们能学到许多汉字、语法结构、中国历史知识和儒家道义，特别是孝道和敬老。

1.2.2.2 Passage

rén zhī chū xìng běn shàn
人之初,性本善。

At the beginning of life, man is good in nature.

xìng xiāng jìn xí xiāng yuǎn
性相近,习相远。

Human nature is alike, but habits make them different.

gǒu bù jiào xìng nǎi qiān
苟不教,性乃迁。

For lack of education, the nature is in alteration.

jiào zhī dào guì yǐ zhuān
教之道,贵以专。

Focus is important for teachers.

xī mèng mǔ zé lín chǔ
昔孟母,择邻处。

Once, Mencius' mother chose the best neighborhood for her son.

zǐ bù xué duàn jī zhù
子不学,断机杼。

When her son did not study, she cut the threads on the loom.

dòu yān shān yǒu yì fāng
窦燕山,有义方。

Another case is Dou Yanshan, who was wise in family education.

jiào wǔ zǐ míng jù yáng
教五子,名俱扬。

He educated his five sons, and all of them were blessed with fame.

yǎng bù jiào fù zhī guò
养不教,父之过。

If a child was born and grew without education, the father should be blamed.

jiào bù yán shī zhī duò
教不严,师之惰。

Only teaching knowledge without pushing, the teacher should be criticized.

zǐ bù xué fēi suǒ yí
子不学,非所宜。

It is not good that young children just play and learn nothing.

yòu bù xué lǎo hé wéi
幼不学,老何为?

If a child fails to learn, what could he do when getting old?

yù bù zhuó bù chéng qì
玉不琢,不成器。

Without being carved, a jade will not be a work of art.

rén bù xué bù zhī yì
人不学,不知义。

If one does not learn, he will not be civilized.

wéi rén zǐ fāng shào shí
为人子,方少时。

As a child, he should make the best of his time.

qīn shī yǒu xí lǐ yí
亲师友,习礼仪。

He should associate with teachers and friends to learn manners.

xiāng jiǔ líng néng wēn xí
香九龄,能温席。

When Huang Xiang was nine years old, he warmed the mat for his father.

xiào yú qīn suǒ dāng zhí
孝于亲,所当执。

It should be done by everyone who loves and respect his parents.

róng sì suì néng ràng lí
融四岁,能让梨。

When Kong Rong was four years old, he could offer his brothers the bigger pears.

tì yú zhǎng yí xiān zhī
弟于长,宜先知。

Even one is younger, one should love and respect his brothers.

shǒu xiào tì cì jiàn wén
首孝悌,次见闻。

One should love his family before he starts to learn,

zhī mǒu shù shí mǒu wén
知某数，识某文。

including counting and computing, as well as reading and writing.

yī ér shí shí ér bǎi
一而十，十而百，

One times ten is ten. Ten times ten is a hundred.

bǎi ér qiān qiān ér wàn
百而千，千而万。

A hundred times ten is a thousand. A thousand times ten is ten thousand.

sān cái zhě tiān dì rén
三才者，天地人。

There are three essential elements to know: heaven, earth and man.

sān guāng zhě rì yuè xīng
三光者，日月星。

There are three kinds of light: they are from the sun, the moon and stars.

sān gāng zhě jūn chén yì
三纲者，君臣义，

There are three ethical disciplines: that of loyalty between the king and his men,

fù zǐ qīn fū fù shùn
父子亲，夫妇顺。

of love between father and son, and of harmony between husband and wife.

yuē chūn xià yuē qiū dōng
曰春夏，曰秋冬。

There are the spring and the summer, the autumn and the winter.

cǐ sì shí yùn bù qióng
此四时，运不穷。

They are the four seasons, alternating all the year round.

yuē nán běi yuē xī dōng
曰南北，曰西东。

There are north and south, west and east.

cǐ sì fāng yìng hū zhōng
此四方，应乎中。

They are the four directions, viewed from the central position.

yuē shuǐ huǒ mù jīn tǔ
曰水火,木金土。

There are water and fire, wood, metal and earth.

cǐ wǔ xíng běn hū shù
此五行,本乎数。

They are five elements, and they mutually reinforce and neutralize each other.

yuē rén yì lǐ zhì xìn
曰仁义,礼智信。

There are benevolence and righteousness, courtesy, intelligence and loyalty.

cǐ wǔ cháng bù róng wěn
此五常,不容紊。

They are the five human norms, which are regulated in certain terms.

dào liáng shū mài shǔ jì
稻粱菽,麦黍稷。

There are rice, sorghum and beans, wheat, millet and corn.

cǐ liù gǔ rén suǒ shí
此六谷,人所食。

They are six kinds of grain for one to serve as food.

mǎ niú yáng jī quǎn shǐ
马牛羊,鸡犬豕。

There are horses, oxen and sheep, chickens, dogs and pigs.

cǐ liù chù rén suǒ sì
此六畜,人所饲。

They are six kinds of livestock, raised in herds by farmers.

yuē xǐ nù yuē āi jù
曰喜怒,曰哀惧;

There are joy and anger, sorrow and fear,

ài wù yù qī qíng jù
爱恶欲,七情具。

love, hate and desire. They are seven human feelings altogether.

páo tǔ gé mù shí jīn
匏土革,木石金;

There are gourds, pottery and leather, wood, stone and metal.

sī yǔ zhú nǎi bā yīn
丝与竹,乃八音。

Together with strings and bamboo, all these can be made into musical instruments.

gāo zēng zǔ fù ér shēn 高曾祖，父而身；	From his great-great-grandfather，to his great-grandfather，
shēn ér zǐ zǐ ér sūn 身而子，子而孙；	to his grandfather and father，to himself and his son，
zì zǐ sūn zhì xuán zēng 自子孙，至玄曾。	to his grandson and great-grandson，and to his great-great-grandson，
nǎi jiǔ zú rén zhī lún 乃九族，人之伦。	whoever is born into the world will face the nine-layer relation.
fù zǐ ēn fū fù cóng 父子恩，夫妇从；	There should be affection between father and son，as well as love between husband and wife.
xiōng zé yǒu dì zé gōng 兄则友，弟则恭；	Brothers should be kind to each other. The elder's amiable，and the younger respectful.
zhǎng yòu xù yǒu yǔ péng 长幼序，友与朋；	A harmony should be maintained among families as well as friends.
jūn zé jìng chén zé zhōng 君则敬，臣则忠。	Even the king should be cordial，to whom the subjects can be loyal.
cǐ shí yì rén suǒ tóng 此十义，人所同。	These are called the Ten Doctrines that everyone in the world should follow.
fán xùn méng xū jiǎng jiū 凡训蒙，须讲究。	To enlighten the school children，good methods must be taken.

xiáng xùn gǔ míng jù dòu
详训诂，明句读。

The meaning must be correctly grasped, and the syntax clear in mind when kids are learning how to read books.

wéi xué zhě bì yǒu chū
为学者，必有初。

A pupil must start his learning from the very beginning.

xiǎo xué zhōng zhì sì shū
小学终，至四书。

After he has learned the basics, he would learn the Four Books next.

lún yǔ zhě èr shí piān
《论语》者，二十篇。

The first book is *Confucius' Analects*, composed of twenty chapters,

qún dì zǐ jì shàn yán
群弟子，记善言。

which were recorded by his disciples and put together as living doctrines.

mèng zǐ zhě qī piān zhǐ
《孟子》者，七篇止。

The second book is called *Mencius*, consisting of seven sections,

jiǎng dào dé shuō rén yì
讲道德，说仁义。

which highlight moralities, as well as benevolence and righteousness.

zuò zhōng yōng zǐ sī bǐ
作《中庸》，子思笔。

The third book is *The Doctrine of the Mean*, written by Zisi, Confucius' grandson,

zhōng bù piān yōng bù yì
中不偏，庸不易。

who promoted a middle way, in which the common truth exists.

zuò dà xué nǎi zēng zǐ
作《大学》，乃曾子。

Zeng Zi wrote *The Great Learning*, from which one can achieve a great deal.

zì xiū qí zhì píng zhì 自修齐，至平治。	He demonstrated a way to self-improvement from individual life to social affairs.
xiào jīng tōng sì shū shú 《孝经》通，四书熟。	When one has mastered *The Filial Scripture*, together with the Four Books,
rú liù jīng shǐ kě dú 如六经，始可读。	the Six Confucian Scriptures can be for him a new start.
shī shū yì 《诗》《书》《易》， lǐ chūn qiū 《礼》《春秋》。	*The Songs*, *The History*, *The Changes*, and *The Rituals* (*containing 2 books*) and *The Annals*
hào liù jīng dāng jiǎng qiú 号六经，当讲求。	are called the Six Confucian Scriptures, which are needed to be studied thoroughly.
yǒu lián shān yǒu guī cáng 有《连山》，有《归藏》；	There was *Lianshan* in the Xia dynasty, which was called *Guicang* in Shang,
yǒu zhōu yì sān yì xiáng 有《周易》，三易详。	with *Zhouyi* in Zhou, all refer to *The Book of Changes*.
yǒu diǎn mó yǒu xùn gào 有典谟，有训诰；	With the records of the early sages' deeds, and with the regulations and laws,
yǒu shì mìng shū zhī ào 有誓命，《书》之奥。	as well as the decrees and rules, *The Book of History* is hard to read.
wǒ zhōu gōng zuò zhōu lǐ 我周公，作《周礼》。	A sage is called the Duke of Zhou, who drafted the rituals for the country,

zhù liù guān cún zhì tǐ 著六官，存治体。	which recorded the official systems of the six palaces and the composition of the states at that time.
dà xiǎo dài zhù lǐ jì 大小戴，著《礼记》。	Dai and his nephew were two scholars, who annotated *The Book of Rituals*.
shù shèng yán lǐ yuè bèi 述圣言，礼乐备。	By digging from the sages' words, they made others know the regulations and the rites.
yuē guó fēng yuē yǎ sòng 曰《国风》，曰《雅》《颂》。	With the National Morals, and the Grace and the Paeans,
hào sì shī dāng fěng yǒng 号四诗，当讽咏。	*The Book of Songs* is divided into four sections, and each should be chanted and recited.
shī jì wáng chūn qiū zuò 《诗》既亡，《春秋》作。	When the truth of *Songs* faded later, *The Book of History* was compiled,
yù bāo biǎn bié shàn è 寓褒贬，别善恶。	which sets the moral code for state officials, and judges the good from the evil.
sān zhuàn zhě yǒu gōng yáng 三传者，有《公羊》；	Three commentaries have been given to *The Book of History* ever written. And the authors are Gong Yang,
yǒu zuǒ shì yǒu gǔ liáng 有《左氏》，有《穀梁》。	Zuo Qiuming and Gu Liang.
jīng jì míng fāng dú zǐ 经既明，方读子。	After having grasped the classics, one can read the works of other schools,

cuō qí yào, jì qí shì 撮其要，记其事。	not only extracting the essentials, but also learning the incidents by heart.
wǔ zǐ zhě, yǒu xún yáng 五子者，有荀扬；	Five figures should be mentioned of the great masters of thought.
wén zhōng zǐ, jí lǎo zhuāng 文中子，及老庄。	They are Xunzi and Yangzi, and Wenzhongzi, Laozi and Zhuangzi.
jīng zǐ tōng, dú zhū shǐ 经子通，读诸史。	With a thorough understanding of the above mentioned, one can proceed to historical works.
kǎo shì xì, zhī zhōng shǐ 考世系，知终始。	From each phase of historical evolution, one can learn the ups and downs of each reign.
zì xī nóng, zhì huáng dì 自羲农，至黄帝。	There lived Fuxi and Shennong, as well as Xuanyuan.
hào sān huáng, jū shàng shì 号三皇，居上世。	They were called the Three Emperors, living in the ancient times.
táng yǒu yú, hào èr dì 唐有虞，号二帝。	Yao and Shun reigned in the later years, who were called the Two Emperors.
xiāng yī xùn, chēng shèng shì 相揖逊，称盛世。	Both yielded the crown to capable men, and their reigns were called the heydays.
xià yǒu yǔ, shāng yǒu tāng 夏有禹，商有汤。	There lived Yu in the Xia dynasty, and there appeared Tang in the Shang dynasty.

zhōu wén wǔ, chēng sān wáng 周文武，称三王。	Together with King Zhou Wen and his son, they were called the Three Great Kings.
xià chuán zǐ, jiā tiān xià 夏传子，家天下。	After Yu was succeeded by his son, all nations were ruled by one family.
sì bǎi zǎi, qiān xià shè 四百载，迁夏社。	And the Xia dynasty lasted four centuries long, till there was revolution in the country.
tāng fá xià, guó hào shāng 汤伐夏，国号商。	The revolution against Xia was led by Tang, who founded a new dynasty called Shang.
liù bǎi zǎi, zhì zhòu wáng 六百载，至纣亡。	Six centuries had passed before it was overthrown in the reign of Zhou.
zhōu wǔ wáng, shǐ zhū zhòu 周武王，始诛纣。	The Zhou dynasty was founded by King Zhou Wu, who captured and beheaded cruel King Zhou.
bā bǎi zǎi, zuì cháng jiǔ 八百载，最长久。	The Zhou dynasty lasted eight centuries, and it's the longest dynasty in history.
zhōu zhé dōng, wáng gāng zhuì 周辙东，王纲坠。	When the capital of Zhou was moved east, the whole state began to go downward.
chěng gān gē, shàng yóu shuì 逞干戈，尚游说。	Seas of wars broke out everywhere, and politicians ran canvassing about.
shǐ chūn qiū, zhōng zhàn guó 始春秋，终战国。	The East Zhou dynasty began with the Spring and Autumn Period, and ended with the Warring States Period.

wǔ bà qiáng，qī xióng chū 五霸强，七雄出。	Five Dukes ruled in the former period, and seven powers dominated in the latter.
yíng qín shì，shǐ jiān bìng 嬴秦氏，始兼并。	First Emperor of Qin appeared later, and annexed all states into one empire.
chuán èr shì，chǔ hàn zhēng 传二世，楚汉争。	When he was succeeded by his evil son, Chu and Han began to fight for the crown.
gāo zǔ xīng，hàn yè jiàn 高祖兴，汉业建。	When Liu Bang won over Xiang Yu, he, as the founder of the Han dynasty, was called Gaozu.
zhì xiào píng，wáng mǎng cuàn 至孝平，王莽篡。	During the reign of Emperor Xiaoping, Han collapsed with Wang Mang's usurping.
guāng wǔ xīng，wéi dōng hàn 光武兴，为东汉。	The throne was restored by Liu Xiu, who was crowned Emperor Guangwu.
sì bǎi nián，zhōng yú xiàn 四百年，终于献。	The later four-hundred-year period is called East Han, which ruined in the reign of Emperor Xian.
wèi shǔ wú，zhēng hàn dǐng 魏蜀吴，争汉鼎。	Three new states of Wei, Shu, and Wu, tussled fiercely for the throne of Han.
hào sān guó，qì liǎng jìn 号三国，迄两晋。	They were called the Three States, to be replaced by two Jin dynasties in chains of wars.

sòng qí jì liáng chén chéng
宋齐继，梁陈承。

Song and Qi rose one after another, and Liang and Chen succeeded later.

wéi nán cháo dū jīn líng
为南朝，都金陵。

They were called the South dynasties as a whole, with their capitals all in Jinling city.

běi yuán wèi fēn dōng xī
北元魏，分东西。

Yuan founded in the north a reign of Wei, splitting into two sections, the east and the west.

yǔ wén zhōu yǔ gāo qí
宇文周，与高齐。

West Wei was renamed North Zhou by Yuwen Jue; East Wei was dominated by Gao Yang with the title of North Qi.

dài zhì suí yī tǔ yǔ
迨至隋，一土宇。

Not until the foundation of the Sui dynasty was there a whole united country.

bù zài chuán shī tǒng xù
不再传，失统绪。

The throne was succeeded by his son, who lost his life and his crown lastly.

táng gāo zǔ qǐ yì shī
唐高祖，起义师。

Li Yuan, with an imperial tile of Tanggaozu, rose up with his army.

chú suí luàn chuàng guó jī
除隋乱，创国基。

He swept off the riots and chaos, and founded the Tang dynasty.

èr shí chuán sān bǎi zǎi
二十传，三百载。

With a succession of twenty emperors, Tang lasted for three hundred years.

liáng miè zhī guó nǎi gǎi
梁灭之，国乃改。

After that the reign of Later Liang rose, which replaced the reign of Tang.

liáng táng jìn jí hàn zhōu 梁 唐 晋，及 汉 周。	Later Liang, Later Tang, Later Jin, and Later Han and Later Zhou,
chēng wǔ dài jiē yǒu yóu 称 五 代，皆 有 由。	are called the Five Dynasties altogether, each replacing the former.
yán sòng xīng shòu zhōu shàn 炎 宋 兴，受 周 禅。	General Zhao, stood out, noble and strong, and the emperor of Zhou handed over his crown.
shí bā chuán nán běi hùn 十 八 传，南 北 混。	Zhao founded the Song dynasty, with eighteen successors, and the capital was moved southward in war riots.
liáo yǔ jīn dì hào fēn 辽 与 金，帝 号 纷。	Two tribes called Liao and Jin, respectively founded their imperial reigns at the same time.
dài miè liáo sòng yóu cún 迨 灭 辽，宋 犹 存。	While Liao and Jin had each its throne, when Jin took Liao, Song lingered on.
zhì yuán xīng jīn xù xiē 至 元 兴，金 绪 歇。	Then Yuan came up, and Jin was stopped. With that Song from history dropped.
yǒu sòng shì yī tóng miè 有 宋 世，一 同 灭。	The latter was subverted by the dynasty of Yuan, and Song also ended in Yuan's invasion.
bìng zhōng guó jiān róng dí 并 中 国，兼 戎 狄。	Yuan conquered the whole country, as well as the remote nationalities.

jiǔ shí nián guó zuò fèi
九十年,国祚废。

After a reign of ninety years, the throne collapsed in rebellions.

míng tài zǔ jiǔ qīn shī
明太祖,久亲师。

Zhu Yuanzhang, the emperor of the Ming dynasty, had been personally leading the expedition.

chuán jiàn wén fāng sì sì
传建文,方四祀。

He made Jianwen inherit the throne, which was seized by Zhu Di only four years later.

qiān běi jīng yǒng lè sì
迁北京,永乐嗣。

When Zhu Di took the throne, the capital moved to Beijing and changed the title of the reigning dynasty to Yongle.

dài chóng zhēn méi shān shì
迨崇祯,煤山逝。

When Chongzhen was in power, the country collapsed, then he killed his daughters and concubines before killing himself in the coal hill.

qīng tài zǔ yīng jǐng mìng
清太祖,膺景命。

Qing Taizu founded a new nation, to fulfill the missions from the heaven.

jìng sì fāng kè dà dìng
靖四方,克大定。

He swept away all the enemies, and unified the whole country.

zhì shì zǔ nǎi dà tóng
至世祖,乃大同。

When Shizu succeeded to the throne, the whole country became an ideal one.

shí èr shì qīng zuò zhōng
十二世,清祚终。

Twelve emperors came to power successively before the fall of the Qing dynasty, which ended with the abdication of Emperor Xuantong.

dú shǐ zhě kǎo shí lù 读史者，考实录。	In studies of historical works, one should delve into the actual records,
tōng gǔ jīn ruò qīn mù 通古今，若亲目。	by which to grasp the history overall, as if shown before one's own eyes.
kǒu ér sòng xīn ér wéi 口而诵，心而惟。	One can learn by reading and chanting, and by way of meditation.
zhāo yú sī xī yú sī 朝于斯，夕于斯。	One should indulge in studies from morning till night.
xī zhòng ní shī xiàng tuó 昔仲尼，师项橐。	Confucius set a good example, who once followed Xiang Tuo as a disciple.
gǔ shèng xián shàng qín xué 古圣贤，尚勤学。	All sages and nobles in ancient times could work hard at their studies.
zhào zhōng lìng dú lǔ lùn 赵中令，读《鲁论》。	A prime minister called Zhao Pu lost himself in the study of *The Analects*.
bǐ jì shì xué qiě qín 彼既仕，学且勤。	Though he had a high post in the government, he was still a diligent learner.
pī pú biān xiāo zhú jiǎn 披蒲编，削竹简。	Lu Wenshu copied books on cattail leaves, and Gong Sunhong wrote on bamboo chips.
bǐ wú shū qiě zhī miǎn 彼无书，且知勉。	The poor guys had no books of their own, yet they had such means to try.
tóu xuán liáng zhuī cì gǔ 头悬梁，锥刺股。	Sun Jing fastened his hair to the beam, and Su Qin stabbed his thighs with an awl.

bǐ bù jiào zì qín kǔ 彼不教，自勤苦。	Why both of them did such strange deeds? They took pains to learn of themselves.
rú náng yíng rú yìng xuě 如囊萤，如映雪。	Che Yin read in the light of glow worms, and Sun Kang used the reflection of snow to read.
jiā suī pín xué bù chuò 家虽贫，学不辍。	Though they came from poor families, they never stopped their studies.
rú fù xīn rú guà jiǎo 如负薪，如挂角。	Zhu Maichen tried reading during firewood cutting, and Li Mi held his book in cattle herding.
shēn suī láo yóu kǔ zhuó 身虽劳，犹苦卓。	Though they were tired out at work, they were still learning hard.
sū lǎo quán èr shí qī 苏老泉，二十七。	Su Xun didn't start to learn until he was twenty-seven.
shǐ fā fèn dú shū jí 始发愤，读书籍。	Though it was late for him to learn, yet he finally had much to attain.
bǐ jì lǎo yóu huǐ chí 彼既老，犹悔迟。	He still felt repentant of starting to learn late, when he was old.
ěr xiǎo shēng yí zǎo sī 尔小生，宜早思。	Young pupils, all of you, had better start learning sooner.
ruò liáng hào bā shí èr 若梁灏，八十二。	Liang Hao was acclaimed at the age of eighty-two.

duì dà tíng kuí duō shì 对大廷，魁多士。	He stood out from the scholars, and was listed top in Court Examination.
bǐ jì chéng zhòng chēng yì 彼既成，众称异。	Only after he had been a success, could others hail to him in surprise.
ěr xiǎo shēng yí lì zhì 尔小生，宜立志。	Young pupils, all of you, had better decide what to do.
yíng bā suì néng yǒng shī 莹八岁，能咏诗。	When Zu Ying was eight years old, he could recite many poems.
mì qī suì néng fù qí 泌七岁，能赋棋。	And when Li Mi was seven, he could compose an ode to chess.
bǐ yǐng wù rén chēng qí 彼颖悟，人称奇。	Such boys with unusual talents always surprise other people.
ěr yòu xué dāng xiào zhī 尔幼学，当效之。	Young pupils, all of you, had better learn from what they've done.
cài wén jī néng biàn qín 蔡文姬，能辨琴。	Cai Wenji was such a gifted girl that she was expert at music.
xiè dào yùn néng yǒng yín 谢道韫，能咏吟。	And Xie Daoyun, a bright young lady, showed her poetic gift on a snowy day.
bǐ nǚ zǐ qiě cōng mǐn 彼女子，且聪敏。	There were many girls as such, who were clever and smart.
ěr nán zǐ dāng zì jǐng 尔男子，当自警。	All of you, boys, should be aware of yourselves.

táng liú yàn fāng qī suì 唐刘晏，方七岁。	When Liu Yan, a figure of the Tang dynasty, was at the age of seven,
jǔ shén tóng zuò zhèng zì 举神童，作正字。	he was called a child prodigy, and was in charge of proofreading books for the government.
bǐ suī yòu shēn yǐ shì 彼虽幼，身已仕。	Young as he was, he became an official.
ěr yòu xué miǎn ěr zhì 尔幼学，勉尔致。	All of you, young learners, can also achieve the same.
yǒu wéi zhě yì ruò shì 有为者，亦若是。	Whoever hold such ambition will also succeed like this.
quǎn shǒu yè jī sī chén 犬守夜，鸡司晨。	A dog can keep watch at night, and a rooster can herald the dawn.
gǒu bù xué hé wéi rén 苟不学，曷为人？	If a person fails to learn, how can he be a successful person?
cán tǔ sī fēng niàng mì 蚕吐丝，蜂酿蜜。	A silkworm can make silk, and a honeybee can make honey.
rén bù xué bù rú wù 人不学，不如物。	If a person fails to learn, he will be good for nothing.
yòu ér xué zhuàng ér xíng 幼而学，壮而行。	If a child learns a lot, he will succeed in his adulthood,
shàng zhì jūn xià zé mín 上致君，下泽民。	not only serving the country, but also benefiting the people.

yáng míng shēng xiǎn fù mǔ 扬名声，显父母。	He will run into great fame，which brings honor to his parents.
guāng yú qián yù yú hòu 光于前，裕于后。	All his ancestors will enjoy the glory，and all his offspring will benefit from his victory.
rén yí zǐ jīn mǎn yíng 人遗子，金满嬴。	People usually bequeath their children with boxes of golden bars.
wǒ jiào zǐ wéi yī jīng 我教子，惟一经。	And what I leave to my son is nothing but this scripture.
qín yǒu gōng xì wú yì 勤有功，戏无益。	Study hard，and you'll succeed. Play truant，and you'll fail.
jiè zhī zāi yí miǎn lì 戒之哉，宜勉力。	Be aware of all this，and work harder and harder.

Part Two Chinese Characters

2.1 Basic Knowledge

Chinese characters are involved in Chinese traditional history and culture which has a history of more than 5,000 years. Chinese characters are not only a tool for people to exchange ideas, communicate and spread information, but also a carrier of Chinese culture. While you are learning the pronunciation of Chinese characters, the ability to write Chinese characters in a standard, correct and neat way is not only a basic guarantee for effective written communication, but also an important basis for foreign students to learn Chinese and other courses.

中国五千年源远流长且博大精深的传统文化离不开汉字。汉字不仅是人们交流思想、沟通和传播信息的工具,而且是中华民族文化的载体。在学习汉字发音的同时,能规范、端正、整洁地书写汉字,既是有效地进行书面交流的基本保证,也是外国学生学习中国语文和其他课程的重要基础。

Requirements for "Standard Characters": smooth, generous, beautiful, practical. You should remember Chinese characters correctly before you can write correct Chinese characters. The following is basic knowledge about Chinese characters and rules of writing Chinese characters.

"规范字"要求:流畅、大方、美观、实用。在正确书写汉字前,要正确识记汉字。下面介绍汉字的基本知识和书写规则。

2.1.1 Strokes

2.1.1.1 Basic Strokes

Chinese characters are composed of strokes. Strokes are the movement in writing surface. Strokes are the smallest units in Chinese characters. You should know the strokes and write them according to the order. Strokes are not only the key to write Chinese characters correctly, but also helps you remember Chinese characters.

汉字由笔画构成。笔画是书写的轨迹，是汉字结构的最小单位。应该掌握笔画，并且按照笔顺书写。笔画不仅是写好字的关键，而且还可以帮助识记汉字。

There are 8 basic strokes. Such as:

共有 8 个基本笔画。如下：

No.	Basic Strokes		Types
1	diǎn 点	dot	
2	héng 横	horizontal	
3	shù 竖	vertical	
4	piě 撇	left-falling	
5	nà 捺	right-falling	
6	tí 提	rising	
7	gōu 钩	hook	
8	zhé 折	turning	

Each one can be divided into different types. Here are all the strokes:

每个笔画又可以分为不同的类型。下面是所有的笔画：

No.	Basic Strokes	Types	Names	Examples
1	diǎn 点 dot		zuǒ diǎn 左点 left dot	huǒ bàn 火 办
			yòu diǎn 右点 right dot	liù gē 六 戈
			cháng diǎn 长点 long dot	yáo nán 爻 难
			piě diǎn 撇点 left-falling dot	hǎo 好
2	héng 横 horizontal		duǎn héng 短横 short horizontal	shàng mò 上 末
			cháng héng 长横 long horizontal	cóng qiě 丛 且
3	shù 竖 vertical		xuán zhēn shù 悬针竖 pin vertical	jiǎ zhōng 甲 中
			duǎn shù 短竖 short vertical	bīng zú 兵 足
			cháng shù 长竖 long vertical	xiāng xié 相 协

续表

No.	Basic Strokes	Types	Names	Examples
4	piě 撇 left-falling		píng piě 平撇 flat left-falling	qiān shǒu 千 手
			shù piě 竖撇 vertical left-falling	shuǎi dǎn 甩 胆
			xié piě 斜撇 slant left-falling	rén rù 人 入
			héng piě 横撇 horizontal left-falling	yòu shèng 又 圣
			shù zhé piě 竖折撇 vertical turning left-falling	zhuān [illegible]
5	nà 捺 right-falling		píng nà 平捺 flat right-falling	dào zhī 道 之
			xié nà 斜捺 slant right-falling	rén rù 人 入
6	tí 提 rising		píng tí 平提 flat rising	jí qiǎo 级 巧
			shù tí 竖提 vertical rising	bǐ shì 比 氏
			héng zhé tí 横折提 horizontal turning rising	huà 话

续表

No.	Basic Strokes	Types	Names	Examples
			héng gōu 横钩 horizontal hook	guàn qiàn 冠 欠
			shù gōu 竖钩 vertical hook	liú cùn 刘 寸
			xié gōu 斜钩 slant hook	xì shù 戏 戍
			wò gōu 卧钩 reclining hook	sī 思
			zuǒ wān gōu 左弯钩 left bend hook	shǐ 豕
7	gōu 钩 hook		shù yòu wān gōu 竖右弯钩 vertical right bend hook	máo jiàn 毛 见
			héng zhé gōu 横折钩 horizontal turning hook	tóng nèi 同 内
			héng zhé zhé zhé gōu 横折折折勾 horizontal and three turnings hook	nǎi 乃
			shù zhé zhé gōu 竖折折勾 vertical and two turnings hook	yǔ mǎ 与 马

续表

No.	Basic Strokes	Types	Names	Examples
7	gōu 钩 hook		héng zhé zuǒ wān gōu 横折左弯钩 horizontal turning and left bend hook	lín chén 邻 陈
			héng zhé yòu wān gōu 横折右弯钩 horizontal turning and right bend hook	jiǔ jī 九 几
8	zhé 折 turning		héng zhé 横折 horizontal turning	mǐn kǒu 皿 口
			shù zhé 竖折 vertical turning	jù qū 巨 区
			piě zhé 撇折 left-falling turning	me xì 么 系

2.1.1.2 Rules of Strokes

Besides all above, you must learn rules of the strokes in order to write Chinese characters correctly.

除了以上提到的，还必须学习笔顺规则来正确书写汉字。

Here are some rules of the stroke order.

以下是一些笔顺规则。

NO.	Rules	Examples
1	Write the strokes from the left to the right. 从左到右。	礼：礻 礼 怀：忄 怀
2	Write the strokes from the top to the bottom. 从上到下。	苗：艹 苗

续表

NO.	Rules	Examples
3	Write the horizontal strokes first, then the vertical strokes. 先横后竖。	十:一 十 干:一 二 干
4	Write the left-falling strokes first, then the right-falling strokes. 先撇后捺。	八:丿 八 人:丿 人
5	Write the strokes from the outside to the inside. 先外后里。	闻:门 闻 冈:冂 冈
6	Write the strokes from the outside to the inside, then finish the bottom line of the outside at last. 先外后里,再封口。	回:冂 同 回
7	If the middle part is longer or bigger, you should write the middle strokes, then the left and the right. 当中间部分较长或较宽时,先写中间后写两边。	办:力 办 小:亅 小
8	If the stroke dot is in the upper part or on the upper left, write it first. 正上、左上的点,必须先写。	亢:亠 亢 关:丶 丷 关
9	If the stroke dot is inside the character or on the upper right, write it at last. 里边、右上的点,必须后写。	勺:勹 勺 术:一 十 木 术
10	Write “辶” (walking bottom) and “廴” (jian zi bottom) at last. 最后写“辶”(走之底)和“廴”(建字底)。	迟:尺 迟 廷:壬 廷
11	If the character contains “匚”(fāng), you should write the upper horizontal stroke first, then the inside part, lastly, the “乚”. “匠字框”的字,先写上边一横,再写里边,最后写竖折。	匹:一 兀 匹

续表

NO.	Rules	Examples
12	If the character contains "凵"(kǎn or qiǎn), you should write the strokes inside first, then the outside. "凶字框"的字,先里后外。	凼:水 凼 函:氶 函

2.1.2 Radicals

After learning the strokes, you can write most basic and simple Chinese characters. Next, it is the second feature of Chinese characters: radicals. Radicals are also called sides of a Chinese character (偏旁, pianpang). Some of they are used as the basis for arrangement and retrieval of Chinese characters (部首, bushou). Radicals are the structural units of synthetic characters, and are composed of strokes; some of them (bushou) have the function of matching Chinese characters. Most radicals (bushou) in dictionaries are taken by the ideographic and phonographic sides of Chinese characters.

学习完笔画后,就可以写出大多数基础、简单的汉字。接下来是汉字的第二个特征:偏旁。有些偏旁(部首)用来作为排列和检索汉字的依据。偏旁是合体字的结构单位,由笔画组成,其中的部首具有组配汉字的功能。字典中大多数部首是由汉字中具有表意作用和发音作用的偏旁充当的。

Generally, radicals are in the upper, lower, left or right positions of Chinese characters. If it is on the top, we call it the top or the head. If it is on the bottom, we call it the bottom. If it is on the left or right, we call it the side (no matter left or right). In addition, there are some radicals that are enclosed forms, and we call them frames. Such as:

一般偏旁位于汉字的上、下、左、右位置。如果处于上部,我们称之为头;如果处于下部,我们称之为底;如果处于左边和右边,我们称之为旁(无论左右)。另外,还有一些偏旁是包围形式的,我们称之为框,如:

head: 草 宝

bottom: 热 竖

left side: 打 说

right side: 割 数

Some radicals have meanings, such as the "plant head (草字头, caozi head)". Almost all Chinese characters that contain the radical "plant head" having a meaning related to plants, because "cao" is a kind of plant, so this radical represents plants. Another example is the " fire side", almost all the Chinese characters containing the "fire side" are associated with the meaning of high temperature. Such as:

有的偏旁有含义，比如草字头。几乎所有含草字头的汉字，其意义都跟植物相关，因为草是一种植物，所以草字头这个偏旁就表示该字和植物有关。再如火字旁，几乎所有含火字旁的汉字都跟高温相关。如：

花菜 莲花 | 火焰 烟灰

Some radicals have no meaning, we only translate it from the pronunciation of Chinese characters. Such as:

有些偏旁没有含义。如：

赵 参

The following is all the radicals.

以下是所有的偏旁。

Stroke Number	Examples
一画 One stroke	丨亅丿乛一乙乚丶
二画 Two strokes	八勹匕冫卜厂刀刂儿二 匚阝丷几卩冂力冖凵人 亻入十厶亠匸讠廴又
三画 Three strokes	艹屮彳巛川辶寸大飞干 工弓廾广丬⺌ 己彐彑巾口马 门宀女犭山彡尸饣士扌已 氵纟巳土囗兀夕小忄幺 弋尢夂子

续表

Stroke Number	Examples
四画 Four strokes	贝比灬长车歹斗厄方风⺗ 父戈丬户火旡见斤耂毛爪 木肀牛牜 爿片支夂气欠龵 犬日氏礻手殳水瓦冘王冃 韦文毋心牙爻曰月爫支止
五画 Five strokes	白癶歺甘瓜禾钅立龙矛氺 皿母目疒鸟皮生石矢示立 罒田玄穴疋业衤用玉⺪
六画 Six strokes	耒艸老臣虫而耳缶艮虍臼 ⺷𦍌米齐肉色舌覀页先行血 羊聿至舟衣竹自羽糸糹
七画 Seven strokes	貝采镸辰赤豆谷見角克里車辵 卤麦身豕辛言邑酉豸走足
八画 Eight strokes	青雨齿非阜金隶鱼隹長面釒門飠
九画 Nine strokes	革骨鬼韭面首香音頁
十画 Ten strokes	髟高鬲馬門
十一画 Eleven strokes	黄鹵鹿麻魚
十二画 Twelve strokes	鼎黑黍
十三画 Thirteen strokes	鼓鼠

续表

Stroke Number	Examples
十四画 Fourteen strokes	鼻
十五画 Fifteen strokes	龍

In fact, there are only 58 radicals commonly used. Here are all of them.
事实上,常用的偏旁只有 58 个。以下全部列出。

Stroke Number	Radicals	Names	Examples
二画	厂	piān chǎng tóu 偏 厂 头 partial changzi head	tīng lì hòu 厅 历 厚
	匚	qū zì kuàng 区 字 框 quzi frame	qū jiàng xiá 区 匠 匣
	刂	lì dāo páng 立 刀 旁 knife side	liè bié jiàn 列 别 剑
	冂	tóng zì kuàng 同 字 框 tongzi frame	gāng wǎng zhōu 冈 网 周
	亻	dān rén páng 单 人 旁 single-person side	rén wèi nǐ 仁 位 你
	勹	bāo zì tóu 包 字 头 baozi head	sháo gōu xún 勺 勾 旬
	亠	jīng zì tóu 京 字 头 jingzi head	liù jiāo hài 六 交 亥
	冫	liǎng diǎn shuǐ páng 两 点 水 旁 two-drops-water side	cì lěng zhǔn 次 冷 准

续表

Stroke Number	Radicals	Names	Examples
二画	冖	tū bǎo gài 秃 宝 盖 cap-without-dot head	xiě jūn guàn 写 军 冠
	讠	yán zì páng 言 字 旁 symbolic language side	jì lùn shī 计 论 诗
	卩	dān ěr páng 单 耳 旁 single-ear side	wèi yìn què 卫 印 却
	阝	shuāng ěr páng 双 耳 旁 double-ear side	fáng zǔ nà 防 阻 那
	厶	sī zì páng tóu dǐ 私 字 旁/头/底 sizi side/head/bottom	yǔn qù yǐ 允 去 矣
	廴	jiàn zhī páng dǐ 建 之 旁/底 jianzi side/bottom	yán tíng jiàn 延 廷 建
三画	土	tí tǔ páng 提 土 旁 soil side	dì chǎng chéng 地 场 城
	扌	tí shǒu páng 提 手 旁 hand side	káng dān zhāi 扛 担 摘
	艹	cǎo zì tóu 草 字 头 plant head	ài huā yīng 艾 花 英
	廾	nòng zì dǐ 弄 字 底 nongzi bottom	kāi biàn yì 开 弁 异
	尢	yóu zì páng 尤 字 旁 youzi side	yóu lóng wú 尤 龙 无
	囗	guó zì kuàng 国 字 框 guozi frame	yīn guó tú 因 国 图

续表

Stroke Number	Radicals	Names	Examples
三画	彳	shuāng rén páng 双人旁 double-person side	háng zhēng tú 行 征 徒
	彡	sān piě páng 三撇旁 three-left-falling side	xíng cān xū 形 参 须
	犭	fǎn quǎn páng 反犬旁 animal side	gǒu māo zhū 狗 猫 猪
	夂	zhé wén páng 折文旁 turning-wen side	chù dōng xià 处 冬 夏
	饣	shí zì páng 食字旁 food side	yǐn sì shì 饮 饲 饰
	丬(爿)	jiàng zì páng 将字旁 jiangzi side	zhuàng zhuàng kē 状 壮 牁
	广	guǎng zì páng 广字旁 guangzi side	zhuāng diàn xí 庄 店 席
	氵	sān diǎn shuǐ páng 三点水旁 three-drops-water side	jiāng wāng huó 江 汪 活
	忄	shù xīn páng 竖心旁 vertical-heart side	huái kuài xìng 怀 快 性
	宀	bǎo gài tóu 宝盖头 cap head	yǔ dìng bīn 宇 定 宾
	辶	zǒu zhī dǐ 走之底 walking bottom	guò hái sòng 过 还 送
	子	zǐ zì páng 子字旁 children side	kǒng sūn hái 孔 孙 孩

续表

Stroke Number	Radicals	Names	Examples
三画	纟	jiǎo sī páng 绞丝旁 silk side	hóng yuē chún 红 约 纯
	巛	sān guǎi tóu 三拐头 three-turning head	zāi yōng cháo 甾 邕 巢
四画	王	wáng zì páng 王字旁 king side	wán zhēn bān 玩 珍 班
	木	mù zì páng 木字旁 wood side	pǔ dù dòng 朴 杜 栋
	牜	niú zì páng 牛字旁 bull side	mǔ wù shēng 牡 物 牲
	攵	fǎn wén páng 反文旁 inverse-wen side	shōu zhèng jiào 收 政 教
	爫	zhǎo zì tóu 爪字头 zhaozi head	tuǒ shòu yǎo 妥 受 舀
	火	huǒ zì páng 火字旁 fire side	dēng càn zhú 灯 灿 烛
	灬	sì diǎn dǐ 四点底 four-point bottom	jié diǎn rè 杰 点 热
	礻	shì zì páng 示字旁 god side	lǐ shè zǔ 礼 社 祖
五画	𡗗	chūn zì tóu 春字头 chunzi head	fèng zòu qín 奉 奏 秦
	罒	sì zì tóu 四字头 sizi head	luó bà zuì 罗 罢 罪

续表

Stroke Number	Radicals	Names	Examples
五画	皿	mǐn zì dǐ 皿 字 底 utensil bottom	yú yì kuī 盂 益 盔
	钅	jīn zì páng 金 字 旁 gold side	gāng qīn líng 钢 钦 铃
	禾	hé mù páng 禾 木 旁 herb side	hé qiū zhǒng 和 秋 种
	疒	bìng zì páng 病 字 旁 illness side	zhèng téng hén 症 疼 痕
	衤	yī zì páng 衣 字 旁 fabric side	chū xiù bèi 初 袖 被
	癶	dēng zì tóu 登 字 头 dengzi head	guǐ dēng dèng 癸 登 凳
六画	覀(西)	xī zì tóu 西 字 头 xizi head	yào jiǎ piào 要 贾 票
	虍	hǔ zì tóu 虎 字 头 tiger head	lǔ lǜ xū 虏 虑 虚
	⺮(竹)	zhú zì tóu 竹 字 头 bamboo head	xiào bǐ dí 笑 笔 笛
	𦍌	yáng zì páng 羊 字 旁 sheep side	chà líng jié 差 羚 羯
	龹	juàn zì tóu 卷 字 头 juanzi head	quàn quán juàn 券 拳 眷
	米	mǐ zì páng 米 字 旁 rice side	fěn liào liáng 粉 料 粮

续表

Stroke Number	Radicals	Names	Examples
七画	⻊	zú zì páng 足 字 旁 foot side	yuè jù tī 跃 距 踢
八画	髟	máo zì tóu 髦 字 头 hair head	máo rán bìn 髦 髯 鬓

2.1.3 Structures

The third feature of Chinese characters is the Stroke Pattern (Structure). When learning how to write Chinese characters, you should follow the structure order of Chinese characters to write correctly in addition to pay attention to the stroke sequence. So, you need to learn the structure and its order.

汉字的第三个特点是间架结构。在学习书写汉字时，除了要注意笔顺外，还要按汉字的结构顺序来规范书写，所以需要认识汉字的间架结构及其顺序。

The structures of Chinese characters are divided into two types: the single and the combined.

汉字结构分为两种：独体和合体。

Single characters are those which cannot be separated into two or more than two parts.

独体字是指那些无法分离出两个或两个以上部件的汉字。

Here are some examples of single characters:

以下是一些独体字的例子：

guǎng 广	shǒu 手	hé 禾	dōng 东	xī 西	sān 三

Combined characters are those which are made up of two or more than two parts. And the combined can be divided into several different structures.

合体字为由两个或两个以上部件组成的汉字。合体字有不同的结构。

Here are the commonly used structures and writing orders of the combined:

以下列出了常用的合体字结构及其书写顺序：

Structures	Examples		Rules
Up-down structure 上下结构		cài sī lǐ 菜 思 李	Write from the top to the bottom. 从上到下。
		shuāng yào sù 霜 药 宿	
		xiǎng mào rǎn 想 贸 染	
Up-middle-down structure 上中下结构		màn jiù gōng 曼 舅 宫	Write from the top to the middle, then to the bottom. 从上到中至下。
Left-right structure 左右结构		xiū dǎ cháo 休 打 朝	Write from the left to the right. 从左到右。
Left-middle-right structure 左中右结构		xiè jiē hóng 谢 街 鸿	Write from the left to the middle, then to the right. 从左到中至右。
All-enclosed structure 全包围结构		guó tuán yuán 国 团 圆	Write from the outside to the inside, then finish the bottom line of the outside at the end. 先外后里，再封口。

续表

Structures	Examples	Rules
Bi-enclosed structure 两面包围结构	bìng ní páng 病 尼 庞	Write the first two from the outside to the inside, but the last one from the inside to the outside. 前两种结构先外后里，最后一种结构先里后外。
	sī kě xí 司 可 习	
	dào qù yán 道 趣 延	
Tri-enclosed structure 三包围结构	tóng wèn xiàng 同 问 向	Write from the outside to the inside. 先外后里。
	shān xiōng hán 山 凶 函	Write from the middle to the left, then to the right. 先中间，再从左到右。
	kuāng qū yī 匡 区 医	Write the top line first, then the middle part, the vertical stroke, the bottom line at the end. 先上后里，再从左往下封口。
Interwoven structure 穿插结构	chéng è wū 乘 噩 巫	Write from the top to the middle, then to the bottom. 从上到中。
Three-part structure 品字结构	pǐn sēn zhòng 品 森 众	Write from the top to the bottom, then write the bottom from left to right. 先上后下。

More words about some Chinese characters with bi- & tri-enclosed structures.

详述一下两包围及三包围汉字的书写规则。

Rules	Examples
Write the characters in the semi-enclosed structure of the upper-right or the upper-left from the outside to the inside. 上右和上左包围结构的字，先外后里。	tīng 厅 zuò 座 wū 屋 xún 旬
Write the characters in the semi-enclosed structure of the lower-left from the inside to the outside. 左下包围结构的字，先里后外。	yuǎn 远 jiàn 建 tíng 廷
Write the characters in the tri-enclosed structure of the lower-left-right from the inside to the outside. 左下右包围结构的字，先里后外。	xiōng 凶 huà 画
Write the characters in the tri-enclosed structure of the upper-left-right from the outside to the inside. 左上右包围结构的字，先外后里。	tóng 同 yòng 用 fēng 风
Write the characters in the tri-enclosed structure of the left-enclosing from the upper to the inside, then the lower left. 上左下包围结构的字，先上后里再左下。	yī 医 jù 巨 jiàng 匠 qū 区

2.1.4 Mats

Mats are templates used to standardize the writing format of Chinese characters, including four borders and horizontal and vertical center lines. It is necessary to gradually standardize the writing of Chinese characters in mats.

田字格是一种用于规范汉字书写的模板，包括四条边框和横中线、竖中线。习字时须在田字格中逐渐将汉字写规范。

甲	申	呵	电	号	田	由	史	只	央	兕
叫	另	叨	叹	四	生	失	禾	丘	付	仗
仙	们	仪	甶	仔	他	斥	本	乎	坐	令
甩	印	乐	甸	匆	册	犯	外	处	冬	鸟
包	饥	主	市	立	闪	兰	半	汁	汇	头
宁	宋	它	讨	写	让	礼	训	必	议	讯

上	上	上	上	上	上						
下	下	下	下	下	下						
左	左	左	左	左	左						
右	右	右	右	右	右						

2.1.5 Punctuation

Punctuation is a set of written marks used to indicate sentence reading and mood. They assist the writing, and they are an organic part of the written language, used to express the pause, the mood and the nature and function of words.

标点符号用于标明句读和语气，是辅助文字记录的符号，是书面语的有机组成部分，用来表示停顿、语气以及词语的性质和作用。

The main punctuation marks are as follows:

主要的标点符号如下：

Punctuation		Translation
句号	。	full stop
逗号	，	comma
顿号	、	pause
分号	；	semicolon
冒号	：	colon
书名号	《 》	book-title marks
引号	“ ”	quotation marks
省略号	……	suspension points
感叹号	！	exclamation mark
问号	？	question mark

Here is the function of some punctuation marks.

以下是一些标点的用法。

Punctuation		Function
diǎn hào 点号	jù hào 句号	A full stop is a pause at the end of a narrative sentence. It is used at the end of a sentence. 句号表示一句叙述语气的话完了后的停顿，用在句子末尾。
diǎn hào 点号	dòu hào 逗号	A comma indicates a pause in the middle of a sentence, where the various clauses in between require a pause. 逗号表示一句话中间的停顿，用在一句话之间的各个分句需要停顿处。

续表

<table>
<tr><th colspan="2">Punctuation</th><th>Function</th></tr>
<tr><td rowspan="5">diǎn hào
点号</td><td>dùn hào
顿号</td><td>A pause indicates a pause between the parallel words in a sentence.
句子内部并列词语之间的停顿，用顿号。</td></tr>
<tr><td>mào hào
冒号</td><td>The colon indicates a pause after the cue.
冒号表示提示语之后的停顿。</td></tr>
<tr><td>fēn hào
分号</td><td>A pause between the parallel clauses in a compound sentence is marked by a semicolon.
复句内部并列分句之间的停顿，用分号。</td></tr>
<tr><td>gǎn tàn hào
感叹号</td><td>An exclamation mark is a pause at the end of a strong sentence and is used at the end of an exclamation.
感叹号表示一个感情强烈的句子完了之后的停顿，用在感叹句末尾。</td></tr>
<tr><td>wèn hào
问号</td><td>A question mark is a pause at the end of a question.
问号表示一句疑问语气的话完了后的停顿，用在疑问句末尾。</td></tr>
<tr><td rowspan="2">biāo hào
标号</td><td>yǐn hào
引号</td><td>Quotation marks denote the parts quoted in a text or sentence. We use quotation marks to quote what people say.
引号表示文中、句中引用的部分。引用人物所说的话要用引号。</td></tr>
<tr><td>shū míng hào
书名号</td><td>The title of a book，an article，a newspaper，a publication，etc. should be marked by the book-title marks.
书名、篇名、报纸名、刊物名等，用书名号标示。</td></tr>
</table>

2.2 Classification of Chinese Characters (Making of Chinese Characters)

The Chinese language has a long history in human civilization. It is one of the world's oldest written languages. No other language in the world has been so enduring as Chinese characters.

中国文字在人类文明中拥有悠久的历史，是世界上古老的文字之一。世界上还没有任何一种文字像汉字这样经久不衰。

The classification of Chinese characters is extremely complicated. Here are only a few simple ones for your reference. Chinese characters can be roughly divided into six types: Pictograph, Self-explanatory, Echoism, Comprehensive meaning, Similar meaning and Borrow.

汉字的分类极其复杂，以下只列举几种简单的，供大家参考。汉字大概可以分为六种类型：象形、指事、形声、会意、转注、假借。

(1) Pictograph 象形

This method of writing is drawing according to the physical features of the object. The characters, such as 日(the sun), 月(the moon), 山(the mountain) and 水(water), were originally used to depict the patterns of the sun, the moon, the mountain and water, and gradually evolved into the shape of today.

这种字描绘物体的外貌特征，如日、月、山、水等字，最早就是描绘日、月、山、水的图案，后来逐渐演变成今天的字形。

(2) Self-explanatory 指事

This is a way of expressing something abstract, using symbolic or pictographic symbols to represent a character. For example, 人 (a person) is on the surface, that is "上 (up)", and a person is under the surface, that is

“下(down)”.“刃(the blade)” is a point on “刀(the knife)”, meaning here is very sharp, and so on.

这是表现抽象事物的方法,用象征符号,或在象形字上加上符号来表示某个字。如人在其上写作“上”,人在其下写作“下”,在刀口上加一点即为“刃”,表示这里是锋利的刀刃,等等。

(3) Echoism 形声

Echoism characters are composed of two parts. The pictographic part denotes the meaning, and the phonetic part denotes the pronunciation. For example, the pictographic part of “鸠” is “鸟 (a bird)”, meaning “鸠” is a kind of bird; the phonetic part is “九 (jiu)”, meaning “鸠” pronounces “jiu”.

形声字由表示意义的形旁和表示读音的声旁两部分组成。形旁只取其义,不取其音,例如“鸠”字的形旁为“鸟”,表示“鸠”是一种鸟;声旁“九”只取其音,不取其义,表示“鸠”的读音为“九”。

(4) Comprehensive meaning 会意

In this way, two or more characters are used to form one character, and the meanings of these characters are combined into one meaning. For example, “日(the sun)” and “月(the month)” group together, becoming “明(bright)”; “人(a person)” and “言(word)” are combined into “信(faithful)”, meaning a person should keep his word; the combination of “人(a person)” and “木(a tree)” is “休(rest)”, which means a person leaning against a tree, and he/she is having a rest.

这种字由两个或两个以上的字组成,其意义由这几个字的意义合成。如“日”和“月”合在一起,就是“明”;“人”和“言”组合成“信”字,表示人应信守自己说过的话;“人”和“木”合在一起是“休”字,表示人靠着树休息。

(5) Similar meaning 转注

This means two characters that are annotations to each other, meaning the same but with different shapes. For example, in ancient China “考 (now meaning *examination*)” means old, so it is an alternative of “老 (old)”.

转注是两个字互为注释,彼此同义不同形。古时“考”为年老之义,所以“老”“考”通用。

(6) Borrow 假借

This means borrowing a word to express something else. In ancient time, if there is not a character ready to describe something, it can be expressed by borrowing a character that sounds similar to the pronunciation of the thing.

假借就是借用一字去描述别的事物。在古代,如果某事物只有发音而没有现成的字来描述,就可以借用一个发音相同或相近的字来描述。

2.3 Looking up a Chinese Character

Generally speaking, there are three ways to look up a Chinese character.

一般来说，汉字有三种查字方法。

① *If you only know how to pronounce the Chinese character, you can find the initial of the syllable in the* **Syllable Chart** *(listed in alphabetical order), then you will find the syllable there. The number on the right of the syllable is the page number where the first Chinese character with the same syllable is in the text of the dictionary. Just jump to the page, look through the items and find the character you need.*

如果只知道某字的读音，可以在《音节表》(按字母顺序排列)中先找到这个字拼音的首字母，然后找到该拼音，拼音右边的数字即为该拼音所代表的汉字在词典正文开始的页码。接下来，翻到此页码，仔细浏览词典条目，找到所查汉字。

② *If you only know how to write the Chinese character, you can find its radical (bushou) in the* **List of Radicals** *(ranked according to the number of strokes), then you will find a number on the right of the radical. The number is the page number where the characters containing the same radical are in the* **Character Index** *(ranked according to the number of strokes not including the radical's). Look through the index and find the character. The number on the right of the character is the page number where the character actually is in the text of the dictionary.*

如果只知道某字的写法，可以在《部首检字表》的《部首目录》(按部首笔画数排列)先查到该字部首所在页码。接下来，翻到该页，找到该部首，在该部首下再根据笔画找到所查汉字(有同样部首的汉字按除部首外的剩余笔画排列)，右边的数字即为该字在词典正文的页码。

③ *If you cannot tell the radical of the Chinese character, or don't know how to pronounce it, either, you can just look up the character in the* **Stroke Index for Difficult Characters** (*ranked according to the number of strokes*). *The number on the right of the character is the page number where the character actually is in the text of the dictionary.*

如果不知道某字的部首是什么，也不知道该字的读音，可以在《难检字笔画索引》（按汉字笔画数排列）中查找该字，右边的数字即为该字在词典正文的页码。

Part Three
Chinese Cultural Classics

3.1 Ancient Literature

1 礼运大同篇

lǐ yùn dà tóng piān

The Commonwealth of Great Unity

dà dào zhī xíng yě tiān xià wéi gōng xuǎn xián jǔ néng jiǎng xìn xiū mù

大道之行也，天下为公，选贤与能，讲信修睦。

When the Great Dao (perfect order) prevails, the world is like a Commonwealth State shared by all. Virtuous, faithful, wise and excellent people are chosen as leaders. Honesty and sincerity are promoted, and good neighborliness developed.

gù rén bù dú qīn qí qīn bù dú zǐ qí zǐ

故人不独亲其亲，不独子其子。

So people don't just love their own parents, but love children and parents of others.

shǐ lǎo yǒu suǒ zhōng zhuàng yǒu suǒ yòng yòu yǒu suǒ zhǎng guān guǎ gū dú fèi jí zhě jiē yǒu suǒ yǎng

使老有所终，壮有所用，幼有所长，鳏寡孤独废疾者，皆有所养。

The old are cared for until death, adults can find suitable jobs that make full use of their abilities and children are cared, educated, and fostered. Widows and widowers, orphans and the old without children, the disabled and the diseased can all get good care.

nán yǒu fèn nǚ yǒu guī
男有分，女有归。

Every man has an appropriate job in society and every woman has a good family.

huò wù qí qì yú dì yě bù bì cáng yú jǐ lì wù qí bù chū yú shēn yě bù bì wèi jǐ
货恶其弃于地也，不必藏于己；力恶其不出于身也，不必为己。

They hate to see resources being wasted on the ground, but they do not necessarily keep them for themselves. They hate not to make full use of their abilities, and they do not necessarily work for their own interest.

shì gù móu bì ér bù xīng dào qiè luàn zéi ér bù zuò
是故谋闭而不兴，盗窃乱贼而不作。

So there will be no more conspiracies, robberies, thefts and chaos.

gù wài hù ér bù bì shì wèi dà tóng
故外户而不闭，是谓大同。

Therefore, when you go out at night, the door does not have to be closed, and it is safe. This is the world of great unity.

2 lǐ jì dà xué piān 礼记大学篇

The Great Learning

dà xué zhī dào zài míng míng dé zài qīn mín zài zhǐ yú zhì shàn
大学之道，在明明德，在亲民，在止于至善。

What the great learning teaches, is to explain illustrious morality, to renovate the people, and to rely on the highest excellence.

zhī zhǐ ér hòu yǒu dìng dìng ér hòu néng jìng jìng ér hòu néng ān ān ér hòu néng lǜ lǜ ér hòu néng dé
知止而后有定，定而后能静，静而后能安，安而后能虑，虑而后能得。

The key where to rest being known, the object of the dream is then determined. That being decided, a calm peacefulness may be attained to. To that calmness there will succeed a tranquil repose. In that repose there would be careful thought, and that thought will be obeyed by the attainment of the desired end.

wù yǒu běn mò shì yǒu zhōng shǐ zhī suǒ xiān hòu zé jìn dào yǐ
物有本末，事有终始，知所先后，则近道矣。

Everything has roots and ends, and everything has an end and a beginning. Knowing their order is not far from the purpose of the great learning.

gǔ zhī yù míng míng dé yú tiān xià zhě xiān zhì qí guó yù zhì qí guó zhě xiān qí qí jiā yù qí qí jiā zhě xiān xiū qí shēn yù xiū qí shēn zhě xiān zhèng qí xīn yù zhèng qí xīn zhě xiān chéng qí yì yù chéng qí yì zhě xiān zhì qí zhī zhì zhī zài gé wù
古之欲明明德于天下者，先治其国；欲治其国者，先齐其家；欲齐其家者，先修其身；欲修其身者，先正其心；欲正其心者，先诚其意；欲诚其意者，先致其知；致知在格物。

The ancient people who wished to explain illustrious virtue throughout the kingdom, first ordered well their own countries. Wishing to order well their countries, they first regulated their families. Wishing to regulate their families, they first cultivated themselves. Wishing to cultivate themselves, they should rectify their hearts firstly. Wishing to rectify their hearts, they first should be faithful in their minds. Wishing to be faithful in their minds, they first needed to broaden their knowledge. Such extension of knowledge relied on the investigation of things.

wù gé ér hòu zhī zhì zhī zhì ér hòu yì chéng yì chéng ér hòu xīn zhèng xīn zhèng ér hòu shēn xiū shēn xiū ér hòu jiā qí jiā qí ér hòu guó zhì guó zhì ér hòu tiān xià píng
物格而后知至，知至而后意诚，意诚而后心正，心正而后身修，身修而后家齐，家齐而后国治，国治而后天下平。

Things being investigated, knowledge became improved. Their knowledge being improved, their minds were sincere. Their minds being sincere, their hearts were then rectified. Their hearts being rectified, their children were cultivated. Their children being cultivated, their families were well ordered. Their families being regulated, their states were rightly governed. Their states being rightly governed, the whole kingdom was made tranquil and happy.

zì tiān zǐ yǐ zhì yú shù rén yī shì jiē yǐ xiū shēn wéi běn
自天子以至于庶人，壹是皆以修身为本。

From the Son of Heaven down to the mass of the people, all must consider the cultivation of one's moral character the root of everything.

qí běn luàn ér mò zhì zhě fǒu yǐ qí suǒ hòu zhě bó ér qí suǒ bó zhě hòu wèi zhī yǒu yě
其本乱而末治者，否矣；其所厚者薄，而其所薄者厚，未之有也。

It cannot be, when the root is ignored, that what should spring from it will be perfectly ordered. It never has been the example that what was of great importance has been lightly cared for, meanwhile, that what was of light importance has been heavily cared for.

cǐ wèi zhī běn cǐ wèi zhī zhī zhì yě
此谓知本，此谓知之至也。

This is called knowing the root, which is also called the highest wisdom.

3 zhū zǐ jiā xùn 朱子家训

The Parental Instructions of Zhu Xi

lí míng jí qǐ sǎ sǎo tíng chú yào nèi wài zhěng jié jì hūn biàn xī guān suǒ mén hù bì qīn zì jiǎn diǎn
黎明即起，洒扫庭除，要内外整洁；既昏便息，关锁门户，必亲自检点。

Arise at dawn, sprinkling water and sweeping the courtyard and the stairs; the whole room must be orderly and clean. Rest at dusk, checking the closing and locking of doors and windows personally.

yī zhōu yī fàn dāng sī lái chù bù yì bàn sī bàn lǚ héng niàn wù lì wéi jiān
一粥一饭，当思来处不易；半丝半缕，恒念物力维艰。

Whether porridge or cooked rice, remember it is hard to come by; for half a piece of silk or cloth, think of the difficulty in production.

yí wèi yǔ ér chóu móu wú lín kě ér jué jǐng zì fèng bì xū jiǎn yuē yàn kè qiè wù liú lián
宜未雨而绸缪，毋临渴而掘井。自奉必须俭约，宴客切勿流连。

It is better to mend the house before it rains; don't dig a well until you are thirsty. You must be frugal in life; don't linger over the dinner at the party.

qì jù zhì ér jié wǎ fǒu shèng jīn yù yǐn shí yuē ér jīng yuán shū yú zhēn xiū wù yíng huá wū wù móu liáng tián
器具质而洁，瓦缶胜金玉；饮食约而精，园蔬逾珍馐。勿营华屋，勿谋良田。

If tableware is plain and clean, pottery is better than that made of gold or jade. Eating choice food in moderation, vegetables are better than costly delicacies. Do not build fancy houses; do not scheme for fertile land.

……

zǔ zōng suī yuǎn jì sì bù kě bù chéng zǐ sūn suī yú jīng shū bù kě bù dú
祖宗虽远，祭祀不可不诚；子孙虽愚，经书不可不读。

Although our ancestors died a long time ago, the sacrifice cannot be done without piety; although our descendants are foolish, they must read the classics.

jū shēn wù qī zhì pǔ jiào zǐ yào yǒu yì fāng wù tān yì wài zhī cái wù yǐn guò liàng zhī jiǔ
居身务期质朴，教子要有义方。勿贪意外之财，勿饮过量之酒。

You should live frugally and educate your children and grandchildren with uprightness. You mustn't be greedy for wealth that is not yours, and do not drink too much wine.

yǔ jiān tiāo mào yì wú zhàn pián yi jiàn qióng kǔ qīn lín xū duō wēn xù
与肩挑贸易，毋占便宜；见穷苦亲邻，须多温恤。

Bargain you not with pedlars; share your wealth and be nice when you see the poor neighbors and friends.

…

jiàn fù guì ér shēng chǎn róng zhě zuì kě chǐ yù pín qióng ér zuò jiāo tài zhě jiàn mò shèn
见富贵而生谄容者，最可耻；遇贫穷而作骄态者，贱莫甚。

It is the most shameful thing to look like fawning on a rich person; it is the most contemptible thing to assume a proud attitude when meeting someone poor.

jū jiā jiè zhēng sòng sòng zé zhōng xiōng chǔ shì jiè duō yán yán duō bì shī
居家戒争讼，讼则终凶；处世戒多言，言多必失。

Don't take into court your family disputes; unpleasant endings emerge from lawsuits; comport yourself well in society, and restrain loose-tongued improprieties.

wù shì shì lì ér líng bī gū guǎ wù tān kǒu fù ér zì shā shēng qín
勿恃势力而凌逼孤寡；勿贪口腹而恣杀牲禽。

Don't rely on power and force to bully the orphan and the widow; don't slaughter at will animals and poultry to satisfy your appetite.

guāi pì zì shì huǐ wù bì duō tuí duò zì gān jiā dào nán chéng
乖僻自是，悔误必多；颓惰自甘，家道难成。

Egocentric people shall have many regrets. It is hard for slothful people to run a family.

lún yǔ

4 论语

The Analects of Confucius

zǐ yuē xué ér shí xí zhī bù yì yuè hū yǒu péng zì yuǎn fāng lái bù yì lè hū
子曰:“学而时习之,不亦说乎?有朋自远方来,不亦乐乎?
rén bù zhī ér bù yùn bù yì jūn zǐ hū
人不知,而不愠,不亦君子乎?”

Confucius said: “Isn’t it pleasant to study and review what you have learned? Isn’t it also wonderful when friends visit from distant places? If people do not recognize me, it won’t upset me, am I not a gentleman?”

zǐ yuē dì zǐ rù zé xiào chū zé tì jǐn ér xìn fàn ài zhòng ér qīn rén xíng yǒu
子曰:“弟子入则孝,出则弟,谨而信,泛爱众,而亲仁,行有
yú lì zé yǐ xué wén
余力,则以学文。”

The Master said, “When they are in the presence of their parents, they should be filial. When they go out, they should respect and obey the elder, and be careful in their words and deeds; also be honest, trustworthy and quiet. Then, love people widely, and be close to those who are kind. After practicing in this way, if there is still time for further study, they can learn classical knowledge.”

zǐ yuē sān rén xíng bì yǒu wǒ shī yān zé qí shàn zhě ér cóng zhī qí bù shàn zhě
子曰:“三人行,必有我师焉。择其善者而从之,其不善者
ér gǎi zhī
而改之。”

Confucius said: “Among any three people walking, I will find something to learn for sure. Their good qualities are to be followed, and the shortcomings are to be avoided.”

zēng zǐ yuē wú rì sān xǐng wú shēn wéi rén móu ér bù zhōng hū yǔ péng yǒu jiāo ér
曾子曰:“吾日三省吾身:为人谋而不忠乎?与朋友交而
bù xìn hū chuán bù xí hū
不信乎?传不习乎?”

Master Tseng said, “Every day I check myself on these three points: In acting on behalf of others, have I always been faithful to their interests? In intercourse with my friends, have I always been loyal to my words? Have I failed to repeat the concepts that have been handed down to me?"

zǐ yuē wēn gù ér zhī xīn kě yǐ wéi shī yǐ

子曰:"温故而知新,可以为师矣。"

The Master said, "If a man keeps reviewing his former knowledge, so as to be acquiring new, he will be a teacher of others."

zǐ yuē xué ér bù sī zé wǎng sī ér bù xué zé dài

子曰:"学而不思则罔,思而不学则殆。"

Confucius said, "He who learns but not thinking will be bewildered; he who thinks but not learning will be in danger."

zǐ yuē jūn zǐ shí wú qiú bǎo jū wú qiú ān mǐn yú shì ér shèn yú yán jiù yǒu dào ér zhèng yān kě wèi hào xué yě yǐ

子曰:"君子食无求饱,居无求安,敏于事而慎于言,就有道而正焉,可谓好学也已。"

The Master said, "A gentleman will not devote himself to the pursuit of safety and contentment in material life. He will be earnest in what he is doing, and careful in his speech. Besides, he can also ask for guidance and correction from those who have lofty aspirations and behaviors. In this way, he would be a studious person."

zǐ yuē zhī zhī wéi zhī zhī bù zhī wéi bù zhī shì zhì yě

子曰:"知之为知之,不知为不知,是知也。"

The Master said, "Pretending to understand is not the real wisdom."

zǐ yuē zhì zhě bù huò rén zhě bù yōu yǒng zhě bù jù

子曰:"知者不惑,仁者不忧,勇者不惧。"

Confucius said, "The wise are free from puzzle, the benevolent are not worried, and the brave free from fear."

zǐ yuē jūn zǐ qiú zhū jǐ xiǎo rén qiú zhū rén
子曰:"君子求诸己,小人求诸人。"

Confucius said, "The gentleman seeks everything from himself; the mean man seeks everything from others."

zǐ yuē jūn zǐ chǐ qí yán ér guò qí xíng
子曰:"君子耻其言而过其行。"

The Master said, "It is a shame for a gentleman to brag but not to do practical things."

3.2 Ancient Poetry

1

yǒng é
咏　鹅

骆宾王

é é é
鹅，鹅，鹅，
qū xiàng xiàng tiān gē
曲 项 向 天 歌。
bái máo fú lǜ shuǐ
白 毛 浮 绿 水，
hóng zhǎng bō qīng bō
红 掌 拨 清 波。

鹅呀鹅，弯着脖子向天唱着歌。
洁白的羽毛漂浮在碧绿的水面上，红红的脚掌拨动着清清的水波。

Honk, honk, and honk,
With craning necks they sing to the sky clear.
On green waters float their white feathers,
While their red feet paddle under clear waves.

2

mǐn nóng
悯　农

李绅

chú hé rì dāng wǔ
锄 禾 日 当 午，
hàn dī hé xià tǔ
汗 滴 禾 下 土。
shuí zhī pán zhōng cān
谁 知 盘 中 餐，
lì lì jiē xīn kǔ
粒 粒 皆 辛 苦。

农民辛勤种田正当中午，汗水滴滴落入禾下泥土。
谁知道盘中的颗颗饭食，每一粒都是农民的辛苦。
Under the mid-day sun farmers weed with hoes,
With the sweat dripping drop by drop to the soil.
Who knows that the meals and grains in our bowls,
Every morsel of them comes with farmers' hard toil.

3

jìng yè sī
静 夜 思

李白

chuáng qián míng yuè guāng
床 前 明 月 光，
yí shì dì shàng shuāng
疑 是 地 上 霜。
jǔ tóu wàng míng yuè
举 头 望 明 月，
dī tóu sī gù xiāng
低 头 思 故 乡。

那透过窗户映照在床前的月光，好像是一层层的白霜。
仰首看那空中的一轮明月，不由得低下头来沉思，愈加想念自己的故乡。
The silver moonbeams shine before my bed,
Seeming the autumn hoar-frost on the ground.
Up towards the bright moon I raise my head,
And downwards when nostalgia comes around.

4

dēng guàn què lóu
登 鹳 雀 楼

王之涣

bái rì yī shān jìn
白 日 依 山 尽，
huáng hé rù hǎi liú
黄 河 入 海 流。
yù qióng qiān lǐ mù
欲 穷 千 里 目，
gèng shàng yī céng lóu
更 上 一 层 楼。

太阳依傍山峦渐渐下落，黄河向着大海滔滔东流。
要想遍览千里风景，请再登上一层高楼。
Leaning on the mountain the sun glows;
To east the Yellow River seawards flows.
For the desire of having a broader sight,
You need climb up still one more flight.

5

dú zuò jìng tíng shān
独坐敬亭山

李白

zhòng niǎo gāo fēi jìn
众 鸟 高 飞 尽，
gū yún dú qù xián
孤 云 独 去 闲。
xiāng kàn liǎng bù yàn
相 看 两 不 厌，
zhǐ yǒu jìng tíng shān
只 有 敬 亭 山。

群鸟高飞无影无踪，孤云独去自在悠闲。
你看我，我看你，彼此之间两不相厌，只有我和眼前的敬亭山了。
Flocks of birds flew out of sight;
A lonely cloud leisurely went in flight.
Never tired of looking at each other,
Only Mount Jingting and me, the loner.

6

wèn liú shí jiǔ
问刘十九

白居易

lǜ yǐ xīn pēi jiǔ
绿 蚁 新 醅 酒，
hóng ní xiǎo huǒ lú
红 泥 小 火 炉。
wǎn lái tiān yù xuě
晚 来 天 欲 雪，
néng yǐn yī bēi wú
能 饮 一 杯 无？

我家新酿的米酒还未过滤，酒面泛起一层绿泡，红泥烧制的烫酒用的小火炉也已准备好了。

天色阴沉，看样子晚上要下雪，能否留下与我共饮一杯？

Green bubbles cover my newly brewed and unfiltered wine,

With the red clay stove prepared and the fire looks fine.

Seemingly the snow is going to come at dusk outside;

What about staying and drinking a cup of wine inside?

7

jiāng xuě
江 雪

柳宗元

qiān shān niǎo fēi jué
千 山 鸟 飞 绝，

wàn jìng rén zōng miè
万 径 人 踪 灭。

gū zhōu suō lì wēng
孤 舟 蓑 笠 翁，

dú diào hán jiāng xuě
独 钓 寒 江 雪。

所有的山，飞鸟全无踪迹；所有的路，不见人影踪迹。

江上孤舟，渔翁披蓑戴笠；独自垂钓，不怕冰雪侵袭。

No birds among mountains are in flight;

No human traces on roads appear in sight.

Straw hat and cloak, an old man's in a boat alone.

Fishing solely in the river covered with snow.

8

méi huā
梅 花

王安石

qiáng jiǎo shù zhī méi
墙 角 数 枝 梅，

líng hán dú zì kāi
凌 寒 独 自 开。

yáo zhī bù shì xuě
遥 知 不 是 雪，
wèi yǒu àn xiāng lái
为 有 暗 香 来。

墙角有几枝梅花，正冒着严寒独自开放。
为什么远看就知道不是雪呢？因为梅花隐隐传来阵阵香气。
At the wall corner some plum trees grow;
Alone against the cold their blossoms blow.
Even from afar I know they are not the snow;
For faint fragrances through the air flow.

9 寻隐者不遇

xún yǐn zhě bù yù

贾岛

sōng xià wèn tóng zǐ
松 下 问 童 子，
yán shī cǎi yào qù
言 师 采 药 去。
zhǐ zài cǐ shān zhōng
只 在 此 山 中，
yún shēn bù zhī chù
云 深 不 知 处。

苍松下我询问童子，他说师傅采药去了。
他说师傅就在这座山中，可是林深云密，不知道他到底在哪儿。
I ask your lad beneath a pine;
"My master has gone for herbs fine.
He stays deep in the mountain proud;
I know not where, veiled by the cloud."

10 春晓

chūn xiǎo

孟浩然

chūn mián bù jué xiǎo
春 眠 不 觉 晓，

chù chù wén tí niǎo
处处闻啼鸟。
yè lái fēng yǔ shēng
夜来风雨声，
huā luò zhī duō shǎo
花落知多少。

春日气候适合安睡，不知不觉天就亮了，到处可以听见小鸟的欢叫。回想起昨夜的风雨，不知道吹落了多少花儿。

The morn of spring in bed I am lying,
Not waking up till I hear birds crying.
After one night of wind and showers,
How many are the fallen flowers!

11 相思

xiāng sī

王维

hóng dòu shēng nán guó
红豆生南国，
chūn lái fā jǐ zhī
春来发几只。
yuàn jūn duō cǎi xié
愿君多采撷，
cǐ wù zuì xiāng sī
此物最相思。

红豆生长在南方，每逢春天便会发出许多新芽。希望你多采些红豆，因为它最能寄托相思之情。

The red beans grow in southern land;
In spring they burgeon many branches.
Gather them till full in your hand;
They would revive fond memories.

12 鹿柴

lù zhài

鹿 柴

王维

kōng shān bù jiàn rén
空山不见人，
dàn wén rén yǔ xiǎng
但闻人语响。
fǎn yǐng rù shēn lín
返景入深林，
fù zhào qīng tái shàng
复照青苔上。

空寂的山中不见一个人，只听到人说话的声音。
落日余晖映入深林，又照在青苔上。

No wight is seen in the lonely hills round here,
But the human voice and echoes I merely hear.
So deep in the forest the sunset glow can cross,
That it seems to choose to glitter on green moss.

13 山中送别

shān zhōng sòng bié

山中送别

王维

shān zhōng xiāng sòng bà
山中相送罢，
rì mù yǎn chái fēi
日暮掩柴扉。
chūn cǎo míng nián lǜ
春草明年绿，
wáng sūn guī bù guī
王孙归不归？

在山中送走了好友，日落时关上了柴门。
等到明年春草变绿的时候，朋友啊，你还会再来吗？

In hills I saw you off quite late;
At dust I came back and closed my wooden gate.
Next spring when the grass turns green again,
Would you, my friend, return from the plain?

14 宿建德江

xiǔ jiàn dé jiāng
宿建德江

孟浩然

yí zhōu bó yān zhǔ
移舟泊烟渚，
rì mù kè chóu xīn
日暮客愁新。
yě kuàng tiān dī shù
野旷天低树，
jiāng qīng yuè jìn rén
江清月近人。

把小舟停在烟雾缭绕的沙洲，日落时新愁涌上游客心头。
原野空旷，远天比树还低，江水清澈，月光更亲近游人。

My boat is moored near an isle in mist grey;
I am grieved anew to see the parting day.
On the boundless plain trees seem to escape the sky;
In water clear the moon appears so nigh.

15 登乐游原

dēng lè yóu yuán
登乐游原

李商隐

xiàng wǎn yì bù shì
向晚意不适，
qū chē dēng gǔ yuán
驱车登古原。
xī yáng wú xiàn hǎo
夕阳无限好，
zhǐ shì jìn huáng hūn
只是近黄昏。

傍晚时心情不好，独自驾车登上乐游原。
这里夕阳十分美好，只不过已是黄昏。

Feeling gloomy when dusk draws near,
I drive my chariot to the ancient height.
The sunset is boundlessly dear,
Except it is so close to night.

16 塞下曲

sài xià qǔ

卢纶

lín àn cǎo jīng fēng
林暗草惊风,

jiāng jūn yè yǐn gōng
将军夜引弓。

píng míng xún bái yǔ
平明寻白羽,

mò zài shí léng zhōng
没在石棱中。

黑夜林中昏暗,风吹草动,将军在黑夜中搭箭拉弓。

天亮了寻找昨夜射的白羽箭,箭头深深插入巨大的石块中。

In the gloomy forest grass trembles at wind's howl;
The general regards it as a tiger's show.
He shoots and searches for his arrow at daybreak,
Only to find it piercing into a hard rock.

17 望洞庭

wàng dòng tíng

刘禹锡

hú guāng qiū yuè liǎng xiāng hé
湖光秋月两相和,

tán miàn wú fēng jìng wèi mó
潭面无风镜未磨。

yáo wàng dòng tíng shān shuǐ cuì
遥望洞庭山水翠,

bái yín pán lǐ yī qīng luó
白银盘里一青螺。

洞庭湖的水光与秋月交相融合,水面波平浪静就好像铜镜未磨。

远远望去湖中君山一片翠绿,恰似白银盘里托着一枚青青的田螺。

The autumn moon blends in with soft light of the lake;
The smooth surface of water is like an unpolished mirror bright.
Looking far, the island amid the water clear without a ripple,
Looks like a snail on a silver tray.

18 早发白帝城

zǎo fā bái dì chéng

李白

zhāo cí bái dì cǎi yún jiān
朝辞白帝彩云间，
qiān lǐ jiāng líng yī rì huán
千里江陵一日还。
liǎng àn yuán shēng tí bù zhù
两岸猿声啼不住，
qīng zhōu yǐ guò wàn chóng shān
轻舟已过万重山。

清晨告别彩云之间的白帝城，千里外的江陵一日就能到达。

两岸的猿在不停地啼叫，轻快的小舟已驶过万重青山。

Leaving at dawn the White King crowned with colorful cloud,
I have sailed a thousand miles to Jiangling in a day.
With monkeys' cries along the riverbanks,
My skiff has left behind thousands of mountains.

19 枫桥夜泊

fēng qiáo yè bó

张继

yuè luò wū tí shuāng mǎn tiān
月落乌啼霜满天，
jiāng fēng yú huǒ duì chóu mián
江枫渔火对愁眠。
gū sū chéng wài hán shān sì
姑苏城外寒山寺，
yè bàn zhōng shēng dào kè chuán
夜半钟声到客船。

月亮已落下，乌鸦啼叫，寒气满天，江边的枫树与船上的渔火，难抵我独自傍愁而眠。

姑苏城外的寒山古寺半夜里敲钟，钟声传到了我乘坐的客船。

At moonset the crows are crying in the frosty sky;
In the dim light fishing boats and maples sadly lie.

Beyond the city walls, from the Hanshan Temple,
Bells shatter the ship-borne wanderer's dream and midnight still.

20 山行 (shān xíng)

杜牧

yuǎn shàng hán shān shí jìng xié
远上寒山石径斜,
bái yún shēng chù yǒu rén jiā
白云生处有人家。
tíng chē zuò ài fēng lín wǎn
停车坐爱枫林晚,
shuāng yè hóng yú èr yuè huā
霜叶红于二月花。

沿着弯弯曲曲的小路上山,在那生出白云的地方有几户人家。
停下马车是因为喜爱深秋枫林的晚景,枫叶被秋霜染过,艳比二月春花。

I pass by the winding path to the cold hill;
A few cottages appear where the white clouds rise.
I stop my carriage in maple woods to enjoy the scenery;
Frost-bitten leaves look more gorgeous than the February flowers.

21 九月九日忆山东兄弟 (jiǔ yuè jiǔ rì yì shān dōng xiōng dì)

王维

dú zài yì xiāng wéi yì kè
独在异乡为异客,
měi féng jiā jié bèi sī qīn
每逢佳节倍思亲。
yáo zhī xiōng dì dēng gāo chù
遥知兄弟登高处,
biàn chā zhū yú shǎo yī rén
遍插茱萸少一人。

一个人独自在他乡做客,每逢节日会加倍思念远方的亲人。
遥想兄弟们此刻正登高望远,头上插满茱萸只少我一人。

Being a lonely guest in a foreign land,

I long for loved ones more on a holiday.
I know my brothers must, with dogwoods on their heads,
Go climbing and miss me so far away.

22 黄鹤楼送孟浩然之广陵

huáng hè lóu sòng mèng hào rán zhī guǎng líng

李白

gù rén xī cí huáng hè lóu
故人西辞黄鹤楼，
yān huā sān yuè xià yáng zhōu
烟花三月下扬州。
gū fān yuǎn yǐng bì kōng jìn
孤帆远影碧空尽，
wéi jiàn cháng jiāng tiān jì liú
唯见长江天际流。

友人在黄鹤楼前向我挥手告别，繁花似锦的阳春三月他要去扬州。
他的帆影渐渐消失在碧空中，只看见滚滚长江在天边奔流。
My old friend said farewell at the Yellow Crane Tower in the west;
Down to Yangzhou he went in the flowery May mist.
His sail gradually vanished in the boundless blue sky,
Only the Yangtze River continuously rolls by.

23 望庐山瀑布

wàng lú shān pù bù

李白

rì zhào xiāng lú shēng zǐ yān
日照香炉生紫烟，
yáo kàn pù bù guà qián chuān
遥看瀑布挂前川。
fēi liú zhí xià sān qiān chǐ
飞流直下三千尺，
yí shì yín hé luò jiǔ tiān
疑是银河落九天。

香炉峰在阳光的照射下生起紫色烟霞，从远处看去瀑布好似一匹白绢挂在山前。

高崖上飞腾直落的瀑布有几千尺吧，好像银河从天上泻落到人间。

The sunlight streams on the Censer Peak and a wreath of purple mist rises;

Like an upended river the waterfall sounds loud.

Its torrent drops three thousand feet down to the valley floor;

As if the Milky Way fell straight to the earth.

24 回乡偶书

huí xiāng ǒu shū

贺知章

shào xiǎo lí jiā lǎo dà huí
少小离家老大回，
xiāng yīn wú gǎi bìn máo cuī
乡音无改鬓毛衰。
ér tóng xiāng jiàn bù xiāng shí
儿童相见不相识，
xiào wèn kè cóng hé chù lái
笑问客从何处来。

小时离开故乡老后才回，故乡的口音没变，两鬓却已斑白。

孩子们没人认识我这故乡游子，笑着问我从哪里来。

I left home young and return old,
Speaking as then but with hair grown thin.
The children meeting me do not know me.
They smile and ask:"Sir, where do you come from?"

25 绝句

jué jù

杜甫

liǎng gè huáng lí míng cuì liǔ
两个黄鹂鸣翠柳，
yī háng bái lù shàng qīng tiān
一行白鹭上青天。
chuāng hán xī lǐng qiān qiū xuě
窗含西岭千秋雪，
mén bó dōng wú wàn lǐ chuán
门泊东吴万里船。

两只黄鹂在翠绿的柳树间婉转地歌唱，一队整齐的白鹭直冲向蔚蓝的天空。

我坐在窗前，可以望见西岭上堆积着终年不化的积雪，门前停泊着自万里外的东吴远行而来的船只。

Two golden orioles sing amid the willows green.

A flock of white egrets flies into the blue sky.

From my window the snow-crowned western hills are seen.

Beyond the door the east-bound ships at anchor lie.

26 咏柳 (yǒng liǔ)

贺知章

bì yù zhuāng chéng yī shù gāo
碧玉妆成一树高，
wàn tiáo chuí xià lǜ sī tāo
万条垂下绿丝绦。
bù zhī xì yè shuí cái chū
不知细叶谁裁出，
èr yuè chūn fēng sì jiǎn dāo
二月春风似剪刀。

高高的柳树长满了翠绿的新叶，轻柔的柳枝垂下来，就像万条轻轻飘动的绿色丝带。

不知道这细细的嫩叶是谁的巧手裁剪出来的，原来是那二月里温暖的春风，它就像一把灵巧的剪刀。

The slender tree put on jasper all about;

Thousands of branches pend like fringes made of green silk.

But do you know who cut these slim leaves?

The scissor wind of every spring.

27 江南春 (jiāng nán chūn)

杜牧

qiān lǐ yīng tí lǜ yìng hóng
千里莺啼绿映红，

shuǐ cūn shān guō jiǔ qí fēng
水村山郭酒旗风。
nán cháo sì bǎi bā shí sì
南朝四百八十寺，
duō shǎo lóu tái yān yǔ zhōng
多少楼台烟雨中。

江南大地鸟啼声声，绿草红花相映，水边村寨山麓城郭，处处酒旗飘动。南朝遗留下来的四百八十多座古寺，无数的楼台全笼罩在风烟云雨之中。

Orioles sing for miles amid radiant tints of red and green.
By hills and rills wine shop streamers wave in the breeze.
Of the four hundred and eighty splendid temples built in the Southern dynasties,
So many are shrouded in the mist and rain.

28 liáng zhōu cí 凉州词

王之涣

huáng hé yuǎn shàng bái yún jiān
黄河远上白云间，
yī piàn gū chéng wàn rèn shān
一片孤城万仞山。
qiāng dí hé xū yuàn yáng liǔ
羌笛何须怨杨柳，
chūn fēng bù dù yù mén guān
春风不度玉门关。

黄河好似远远地伸到云层，那一座孤城耸立在万仞高山中。不要埋怨羌笛吹起《折杨柳》的悲曲，只因和煦的春风未曾吹到玉门关。

The Yellow River uprises as high as the white clouds.
A lonely town stands amid the soaring peaks.
The Qiang flute, why do you play the sorrow song?
Because the spring wind never blows through the Gate of Jade.

29 清明

qīng míng

杜牧

qīng míng shí jié yǔ fēn fēn
清明时节雨纷纷，
lù shàng xíng rén yù duàn hún
路上行人欲断魂。
jiè wèn jiǔ jiā hé chù yǒu
借问酒家何处有，
mù tóng yáo zhǐ xìng huā cūn
牧童遥指杏花村。

清明时节细雨纷纷飘洒，路上行人个个落魄断魂。

询问哪里买酒消愁，牧童遥指杏花山村。

A drizzling rain falls endlessly in early April,
Travellers along the road are overwhelmed with gloom.
Where can I find a wine-shop to drown my sad hours?
A cowherd points at a distant hamlet nestling amidst apricot blossoms.

30 题西林壁

tí xī lín bì

苏轼

héng kàn chéng lǐng cè chéng fēng
横看成岭侧成峰，
yuǎn jìn gāo dī gè bù tóng
远近高低各不同。
bù shí lú shān zhēn miàn mù
不识庐山真面目，
zhǐ yuán shēn zài cǐ shān zhōng
只缘身在此山中。

从正面、侧面看庐山，山岭连绵起伏、山峰耸立，从远处、近处、高处、低处看都呈现不同的样子。

之所以认不清庐山真正的面目，是因为我自身处在庐山之中。

It's a range viewed from side to side and peaks upwards.
Far and near, high and low, no two parts are alike.
Of Mountain Lu we cannot make out the true face.
For we are lost in the heart of the very place.

3.3 Traditional Festivals

1 yuán xiāo jié 元宵节

The Lantern Festival

yuán xiāo jié wéi měi nián nóng lì zhēng yuè shí wǔ
元宵节，为每年农历正月十五。

The Lantern Festival is on the 15th day of the first lunar month in every year.

jié rì qǐ yuán dōng hàn míng dì shí qī míng dì tí chàng fó jiào tīng shuō fó jiào yǒu
节日起源：东汉明帝时期，明帝提倡佛教，听说佛教有
zhēng yuè shí wǔ rì sēng rén guān fó shè lì diǎn dēng jìng fó de zuò fǎ jiù mìng lìng zhè yī
正月十五日僧人观佛舍利，点灯敬佛的做法，就命令这一
tiān yè wǎn zài huáng gōng hé sì miào lǐ diǎn dēng jìng fó shì zú shù mín yě dōu guà dēng yǐ
天夜晚在皇宫和寺庙里点灯敬佛，士族庶民也都挂灯，以
hòu zhè zhǒng fó jiào lǐ yí jié rì zhú jiàn xíng chéng mín jiān shèng dà de jié rì
后这种佛教礼仪节日逐渐形成民间盛大的节日。

Origin: During the period of the Eastern Han dynasty, the Ming Emperor advocated Buddhism. When he heard that on the 15th day of the first lunar month Buddhist monks admired Buddhist relics and lit lamps to worship the Buddha, the Emperor ordered that night the lanterns should be lit in the palace and temples to honor the Buddha, and the gentry and ordinary people hang lamps, too. Later this Buddhist ritual festival gradually developed into a grand folk festival.

jié rì fēng sú xí guàn chī yuán xiāo cāi dēng mí shuǎ lóng dēng cǎi gāo qiāo wǔ shī
节日风俗习惯：吃元宵、猜灯谜、耍龙灯、踩高跷、舞狮
zi huá hàn chuán
子、划旱船。

Customs: Eating sweet dumplings, guessing lantern riddles, playing with dragon lanterns, walking stilts, playing lion dance, dancing the "land boat" dance.

jié rì yǐn shí yuán xiāo
节日饮食:元宵。

Food: Sweet dumplings.

2 qīng míng jié 清明节
Tomb-Sweeping Day

qīng míng jié yòu jiào tà qīng jié zài zhòng chūn yǔ mù chūn zhī jiāo
清明节,又叫踏青节,在仲春与暮春之交。

Tomb-Sweeping Day is also known as the Ta-Qing (spring outing) Festival. It is at the turn of mid-spring and late spring.

jié rì qǐ yuán qīng míng jié de jì zǔ xí sú jù chuán shǐ yú gǔ dài dì wáng jiàng xiàng jiāo wài tà qīng shí jǔ xíng mù jì zhī lǐ hòu lái mín jiān yì xiāng fǎng xiào yú cǐ rì jì zǔ sǎo mù lì dài yán xí ér chéng wéi zhōng huá mín zú yī zhǒng gù dìng de fēng sú
节日起源:清明节的祭祖习俗,据传始于古代帝王将相郊外踏青时举行"墓祭"之礼,后来民间亦相仿效,于此日祭祖扫墓,历代沿袭而成为中华民族一种固定的风俗。

Tomb-Sweeping Day's custom is worshiping ancestors. It was said that ancient emperors and their attendants would begin with the ceremony of "worshiping ancestors" when they set foot on the outskirts. Later, the people followed suit, and on this day they visited their ancestors' tombs and it gradually became a custom in China.

jié rì fēng sú xí guàn tà qīng sǎo mù zhí shù fàng fēng zheng dòu jī cán huā huì dàng qiū qiān
节日风俗习惯:踏青、扫墓、植树、放风筝、斗鸡、蚕花会、荡秋千。

Customs: Going on a spring outing, sweeping tombs, planting trees, flying kites, cock fighting, silkworm fair, swinging.

jié rì yǐn shí qīng tuán
节日饮食：青团。

Food: Sweet green rice balls.

duān wǔ jié
3 端午节

The Dragon Boat Festival

duān wǔ jié wéi měi nián nóng lì wǔ yuè chū wǔ shì zhōng guó sì dà chuán tǒng jié rì zhī yī
端午节为每年农历五月初五，是中国四大传统节日之一。

The Dragon Boat Festival is celebrated on the fifth day of the fifth lunar month. It is one of the four traditional festivals in China.

jié rì qǐ yuán zhàn guó shí qī de chǔ guó shī rén qū yuán zài nà tiān tiào mì luó jiāng zì jìn yīn tā zhōng jūn ài guó hòu jiāng duān wǔ zuò wéi jì niàn qū yuán de jié rì
节日起源：战国时期的楚国诗人屈原在那天跳汨罗江自尽，因他忠君爱国，后将端午作为纪念屈原的节日。

Origin: Qu Yuan(B. C. 340—B. C. 278), a poet of Chu, devoted himself to his patriotism by drowning himself in the Miluo River on that day, so the Dragon Boat Festival is the day of memorializing him.

jié rì fēng sú xí guàn huá lóng zhōu guà ài cǎo
节日风俗习惯：划龙舟、挂艾草。

Customs: Dragon boat racing, hanging wormwood.

jié rì yǐn shí zòng zi xióng huáng jiǔ
节日饮食：粽子，雄黄酒。

Food: Zongzi, realgar wine.

qī xī jié
4 七夕节

The Double Seventh Festival (Chinese Valentine's Day)

qī xī jié nóng lì qī yuè chū qī yòu míng qǐ qiǎo jié qī qiǎo jié
七夕节：农历七月初七，又名乞巧节、七巧节。

The Double Seventh Festival is celebrated on the seventh day of the seventh lunar month. It is also known as the Qi qiao Festival.

jié rì qǐ yuán yuán yú duì zì rán de chóng bài hòu róng rù niú láng zhī nǚ de chuán shuō chéng wéi xiàng zhēng ài qíng de jié rì
节日起源:源于对自然的崇拜,后融入牛郎织女的传说,成为象征爱情的节日。

Origin: It originated from the worship of nature. Later, it was integrated with the legend of the oxherd and the weaving maid, and became a specified day for lovers.

jié rì fēng sú xí guàn chuān zhēn qǐ qiǎo bài zhī nǚ
节日风俗习惯:穿针乞巧、拜织女。

Customs: That night, facing the moon, women thread seven or nine needles in line with a colourful thread, who finishes first is praised as being clever and deft; worshiping the weaving maid.

jié rì yǐn shí qiǎo guǒ
节日饮食:巧果。

Food: Sweet fried thin pastry.

5 zhōng qiū jié 中秋节 The Mid-Autumn Festival

zhōng qiū jié zài nóng lì bā yuè shí wǔ
中秋节在农历八月十五。

The Mid-Autumn Festival is on the 15th day of the eighth lunar month.

jié rì qǐ yuán yī shuō qǐ yuán yú gǔ dài dì wáng de jì sì huó dòng èr shuō zhōng qiū jié de qǐ yuán hé nóng yè shēng chǎn yǒu guān qiū tiān shì shōu huò de jì jié nóng mín wéi le qìng zhù fēng shōu jiù yǐ zhōng qiū zhè tiān zuò wéi jié rì
节日起源:一说起源于古代帝王的祭祀活动。二说中秋节的起源和农业生产有关;秋天是收获的季节,农民为了庆祝丰收,就以"中秋"这天作为节日。

Origin: One theory is that it originated from the ritual activity by ancient emperors. The other one is it was related with agriculture; since autumn is the harvest season, farmers celebrated it on the mid-autumn day, and it gradually developed into a festival.

jié rì fēng sú xí guàn shǎng yuè chī yuè bǐng
节日风俗习惯：赏月、吃月饼。

Customs: Enjoying the full bright moon, eating moon cakes.

jié rì yǐn shí yuè bǐng
节日饮食：月饼。

Food: Moon cakes.

6 chóng yáng jié 重阳节 The Double Ninth Festival

chóng yáng jié wéi měi nián de nóng lì jiǔ yuè chū jiǔ
重阳节为每年的农历九月初九。

The Double Ninth Festival is on the ninth day of the ninth lunar month.

jié rì qǐ yuán chóng yáng yě jiào chóng jiǔ yì jīng zhōng bǎ jiǔ dìng wéi yáng shù jiǔ yuè jiǔ rì liǎng jiǔ xiāng chóng wèi zhī chóng yáng liǎng yáng xiāng chóng wéi jí xiáng zhī rì
节日起源：重阳也叫“重九”。《易经》中把“九”定为阳数，九月九日，两九相重，谓之“重阳”。两阳相重为吉祥之日。

Origin: Chong Yang is also called “Chong Jiu”. In *The Book of Changes*, “nine” is a yang number (odd number). September 9th means double yang, an auspicious day.

jié rì fēng sú xí guàn chā zhū yú shǎng jú dēng gāo
节日风俗习惯：插茱萸、赏菊、登高。

Customs: Wearing cornels, appreciating chrysanthemums, climbing hills or mountains.

jié rì yǐn shí chóng yáng gāo jú huā jiǔ
节日饮食：重阳糕、菊花酒。

Food: Double-yang cakes, chrysanthemum wine.

7 春节 (chūn jié)

The Spring Festival

chūn jié wéi nóng lì zhēng yuè chū yī
春节为农历正月初一。

The Spring Festival is celebrated on the first day of the first lunar month.

jié rì qǐ yuán guān yú chūn jié de qǐ yuán yǒu zhū duō shuō fǎ yī bān rèn wéi qǐ yuán yú là jì
节日起源：关于春节的起源有诸多说法。一般认为起源于腊祭。

There are several theories about the origin of the Spring Festival. The popular one is it comes from ceremonies honouring ancestors in early winter.

jié rì fēng sú xí guàn shǒu suì bài nián tiē chūn lián fàng bào zhú gěi yā suì qián
节日风俗习惯：守岁、拜年、贴春联、放爆竹、给压岁钱。

Customs: Staying up to see the new year in, paying New Year's calls, pasting up Spring Festival couplets, letting off firecrackers, giving lunar New Year gift money to children.

jié rì yǐn shí là bā zhōu nián gāo jiǎo zi chūn juǎn
节日饮食：腊八粥、年糕、饺子、春卷。

Food: Laba porridge, New Year cakes, dumplings, spring rolls.

Part Four Texts

4.1 Conversations

1. 初次见面 (chū cì jiàn miàn)

1. The first meeting

(大卫和欧文第一次在寝室相遇。)
dà wèi hé ōu wén dì yī cì zài qǐn shì xiāng yù

(David meets Owen for the first time in the dormitory.)

欧文：你好！你也住在这个寝室吗？
ōu wén nǐ hǎo nǐ yě zhù zài zhè gè qǐn shì ma

Owen: Hello! Do you live in this dorm, too?

大卫：是的！我叫大卫，我是汉语专业一班的。你呢？
dà wèi shì de wǒ jiào dà wèi wǒ shì hàn yǔ zhuān yè yī bān de nǐ ne

David: Yes! I am David, and I am a Chinese major in Class One. And you?

欧文：我叫欧文，我也是汉语专业一班的。
ōu wén wǒ jiào ōu wén wǒ yě shì hàn yǔ zhuān yè yī bān de

Owen: I am Owen. I am also a Chinese major in Class One.

大卫：那我们还是同班同学呢。很高兴认识你！
dà wèi nà wǒ men hái shì tóng bān tóng xué ne hěn gāo xìng rèn shi nǐ

David: So we are classmates. Nice to meet you!

欧文：我也很高兴认识你！
ōu wén wǒ yě hěn gāo xìng rèn shi nǐ

Owen: Nice to meet you, too!

词汇 (cí huì) Vocabulary

第一 (dì yī)	*ordinal number* first
寝室 (qǐn shì)	*noun* dormitory, dorm
相遇 (xiāng yù)	*verb* meet
住 (zhù)	*verb* live
在 (zài)	*preposition* in
专业 (zhuān yè)	*noun* major
同学 (tóng xué)	*noun* classmate

课后习题

Exercises

1. 请在括号里写出对应的拼音或汉字。

Please write down the right syllables or Chinese characters in the parentheses.

第一(　　)　相遇(　　)　专业(　　)　同学(　　)

qǐn shì(　　)　zhù(　　)　zài(　　)　chū cì(　　)

2. 根据例子组词。

Combine words according to the example.

Example: 美 (měi) {(美丽) (美好)}

遇 (yù) {(　　) (　　)}　住 (zhù) {(　　) (　　)}　班 (bān) {(　　) (　　)}　认 (rèn) {(　　) (　　)}

3. 用下列所给词语组句。

Complete the sentences with the words given below.

(1)寝室　这个　住在　你　也　吗　?

____

(2)海伦　叫　我。

____

(3)一班　专业　我　汉语　是　的　。

____

(4)你　认识　高兴　很　也　我　!

____

4. 完成对话。

Complete the dialogues.

(1)Q:我是大卫,你也住在这个寝室吗?

A:____________________________________?

(2)Q:____________________________________!

A:我也很高兴认识你!

5. 翻译。

Translate.

(1)我是大卫。

____

(2)我是汉语专业一班的。

____

(3)很高兴认识你。

____

6. 听写。

Dictation.

2. 问路 wèn lù

2. Asking for directions

（大卫想去超市买零食，他向海伦问路。）
dà wèi xiǎng qù chāo shì mǎi líng shí tā xiàng hǎi lún wèn lù

(David wants to go to the supermarket to buy some snacks. He asks Helen for directions.)

大卫：海伦，你知道学校的超市在哪吗？
dà wèi hǎi lún nǐ zhī dào xué xiào de chāo shì zài nǎ ma

David: Helen, do you know where the school's supermarket is?

海伦：我知道。你要去超市吗？
hǎi lún wǒ zhī dào nǐ yào qù chāo shì ma

Helen: I know. Are you going to the supermarket?

大卫：嗯，我想去买一些零食。
dà wèi ǹg wǒ xiǎng qù mǎi yī xiē líng shí

David: Yes, I would like to buy some snacks.

海伦：你先沿着这条路直走，在第一个路口左转，你会看到一家面包店，超市就在面包店的对面。
hǎi lún nǐ xiān yán zhe zhè tiáo lù zhí zǒu, zài dì yī gè lù kǒu zuǒ zhuǎn nǐ huì kàn dào yì jiā miàn bāo diàn chāo shì jiù zài miàn bāo diàn de duì miàn

Helen: First go straight along this road, then turn left at the first crossing, and you will see a bakery. The supermarket is opposite the bakery.

大卫：好的，我知道了。谢谢。
dà wèi hǎo de wǒ zhī dào le xiè xie

David: OK, I see. Thank you.

词汇 cí huì

Vocabulary

想 xiǎng — *verb* want

超市 chāo shì — *noun* supermarket

mǎi 买	*verb* buy
líng shí 零 食	*noun* snack
wèn 问	*verb* ask
zhī dào 知 道	*verb* know
xué xiào 学 校	*noun* school
yán zhe 沿 着	*adverb* along
lù 路	*noun* road
zhí zǒu 直 走	*verb* go straight
zuǒ zhuǎn 左 转	*verb* turn left
miàn bāo diàn 面 包 店	*noun* bakery
duì miàn 对 面	*adjective* opposite

课后习题
Exercises

1. 请在括号里写出对应的拼音或汉字。

Please write down the right syllables or Chinese characters in the parentheses.

超市(　　　)　零食(　　　)　知道(　　　)　学校(　　　)

zhí zǒu(　　)　zuǒ zhuǎn(　　)　duì miàn(　　)　yán zhe(　　)

2. 组词。

Combine words.

xiǎng 想 ( ) ( )　　wèn 问 ( ) ( )　　zhí 直 ( ) ( )　　duì 对 ( ) ( )

3. 用下列所给词语组句。

Complete the sentences with the words given below.

(1)知道　在哪　学校　你　超市　的　吗　？

____

(2)一些　买　去　零食　想　我　。

____

(3)左转　路口　在　第一个　。

____

(4)在　超市　面包店　就　对面　的　。

____

4. 完成对话。

Complete the dialogues.

(1)Q：你要去超市吗？

A：______________________________。

(2)Q：______________________________？

A：超市就在面包店的对面。

(3)Q：在哪里左转？

A：______________________________？

5. 翻译。

Translate.

(1)你要去超市吗？

____

(2)我想去买一些零食。

____

(3)沿着这条路直走。

____

(4)Turn left at the first crossing.

____

(5)The supermarket is opposite the bakery.

____

6. 听写。

Dictation.

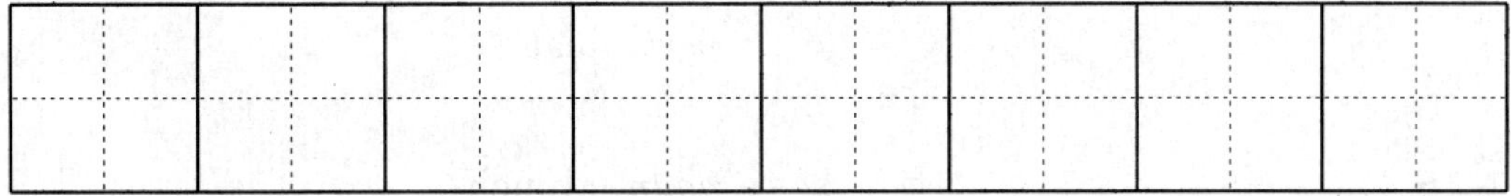

zài shí táng
3. 在食堂

dà wèi hé hǎi lún zài shí táng chī wǔ cān
（大卫和海伦在食堂吃午餐。）

dà wèi hǎi lún nǐ zài chī shén me kàn qǐ lái hěn hǎo chī de yàng zi
大卫：海伦，你在吃什么？看起来很好吃的样子。

hǎi lún zhè shì wǔ chāng yú shì wǔ hàn de tè sè cài nǐ yào cháng yi cháng ma
海伦：这是武昌鱼，是武汉的特色菜。你要尝一尝吗？

dà wèi hǎo ràng wǒ shì yi shì
大卫：好，让我试一试。

dà wèi wa wèi dào hěn bù cuò dàn shì duì wǒ lái shuō yǒu diǎn là
大卫：哇，味道很不错，但是对我来说有点辣。

3. In the canteen

(David and Helen are having lunch in the canteen.)

David: Helen, what are you eating? It looks so delicious.

Helen: This is Wuchang fish, which is Wuhan's specialty. Do you want to have a taste?

David: OK, let me have a try.

David: Wow, it tastes so good, but it's a little spicy for me.

hǎi lún nǐ bù néng chī là ma 海伦：你不能吃辣吗？	Helen: Can't you eat spicy food?
dà wèi duì wǒ bǐ jiào xǐ huan chī tián de 大卫：对，我比较喜欢吃甜的。	David: No, I prefer to eat sweet food.

cí huì **词汇**	**Vocabulary**
shí táng 食堂	*noun* canteen
chī 吃	*verb* eat
wǔ cān 午餐	*noun* lunch
kàn qǐ lái 看起来	*verb* look
hǎo chī de 好吃的	*adjective* delicious
yú 鱼	*noun* fish
tè sè cài 特色菜	*noun* specialty
cháng 尝	*verb* taste
shì 试	*verb* try
là 辣	*adjective* spicy
xǐ huan 喜欢	*verb* like
tián de 甜的	*adjective* sweet

课后习题
Exercises

1. 请在括号里写出对应的拼音或汉字。

Please write down the right syllables or Chinese characters in the parentheses.

食堂（　　　）　午餐（　　　）　特色菜（　　　）　喜欢（　　　）

cháng（　　　）　là（　　　）　yú（　　　）　tián de（　　　）

2. 组词。

Combine words.

chī 吃（　　）（　　）　kàn 看（　　）（　　）　cháng 尝（　　）（　　）　shì 试（　　）（　　）

3. 用下列所给词语组句。

Complete the sentences with the words given below.

(1)样子　看起来　的　很好吃　。

____

(2)武汉　这是　特色菜　的　。

____

(3)对我　有点　来说　辣　。

____

(4)比较　我　甜的　喜欢　吃　。

____

4. 完成对话。

Complete the dialogues.

(1)Q：__________________________________？

A：我在吃武昌鱼。

(2)Q：你要尝一尝吗？

A：____。

(3)Q：你不能吃辣吗？

A：____。

5. 翻译。

Translate.

(1)让我试一试。

____

(2)味道很不错，但是对我来说有点辣。

____

(3)我比较喜欢吃甜的。

____

(4)This is Wuhan's specialty.

____

(5)Helen, what are you eating?

____

6. 听写。

Dictation.

mǎi líng shí
4. 买零食

4. Buying snacks

jīn tiān dà wèi zài jiē wǔ bǐ sài zhōng huò
(今天，大卫在街舞比赛中获
dé le yī děng jiǎng wèi le qìng zhù tā
得了一等奖。为了庆祝，他
qǐng péng yǒu men qù biàn lì diàn mǎi
请朋友们去便利店买
líng shí
零食。)

(Today, David wins the first prize in the street dance competition. To celebrate it, he invites his friends to the convenience store to buy snacks.)

dà wèi jīn tiān wǒ qǐng kè 大卫：今天我请客.	David: It is my treat today.
hǎi lún xiè xie wǒ yào yī dà bāo shǔ piàn hái yǒu yī bēi nǎi chá 海伦：谢谢。我要一大包薯片，还有一杯奶茶。	Helen: Thank you so much. I want a big bag of potato chips and a cup of milk tea.
ān nà wǒ yě yào hē nǎi chá wǒ hái yào yī hé qiǎo kè lì táng 安娜：我也要喝奶茶，我还要一盒巧克力糖。	Anna: I want milk tea, too. Besides, I want a box of chocolates.
ōu wén nà wǒ jiù yào yī gè bīng jī líng 欧文：那我就要一个冰激凌。	Owen: And I will have an ice cream.
dà wèi nǐ hǎo jié zhàng 大卫：你好，结账。	David: Hello, check out.
diàn yuán shǔ piàn shí yuán nǎi chá shí wǔ yuán qiǎo kè lì èr shí bā yuán bīng jī líng bā yuán yī gòng liù shí yī yuán 店员：薯片十元，奶茶十五元，巧克力二十八元，冰激凌八元，一共六十一元。	Clerk: The potato chips are ten yuan, two milk teas are fifteen yuan, the chocolates are twenty-eight yuan, and the ice cream is eight yuan. That is sixty-one yuan in total.
dà wèi hǎo de gěi nǐ qī shí yuán 大卫：好的，给你七十元。	David: OK. Here is seventy yuan.
diàn yuán qǐng nín ná hǎo jiǔ yuán zhǎo líng huān yíng xià cì guāng lín 店员：请您拿好九元找零，欢迎下次光临。	Clerk: Here's your change, nine yuan. Welcome to come next time.

cí huì 词汇 Vocabulary

bǐ sài 比赛	*noun* competition
qǐng kè 请客	*verb* treat

shǔ piàn 薯 片	*noun*	potato chips
nǎi chá 奶 茶	*noun*	milk tea
qiǎo kè lì 巧 克 力	*noun*	chocolate
bīng jī líng 冰 激 凌	*noun*	ice cream
jié zhàng 结 账	*verb*	check out
yuán 元	*noun*	yuan (the unit of money in China)
zhǎo líng 找 零	*noun*	change

课后习题
Exercises

1. 请在括号里写出对应的拼音或汉字。

Please write down the right syllables or Chinese characters in the parentheses.

比赛(　　　)　获得(　　　)　庆祝(　　　)　请客(　　　)

yuán(　　　)　jié zhàng(　　　)

bīng jī líng(　　　)　nǎi chá(　　　)

2. 组词。

Combine words.

huò 获 {(　　) (　　)}　qìng 庆 {(　　) (　　)}　jié 结 {(　　) (　　)}　nǎi 奶 {(　　) (　　)}

3. 用下列所给词语组句。

Complete the sentences with the words given below.

(1)街舞　大卫　获得　在　一等奖　比赛中　了　。

____

(2)九元　拿好　找零　您　请　。

____

(3)零食　朋友们　他　便利店　请　去　买　。

____

(4)还　我　巧克力糖　要　一盒　。

____

4. 完成对话。

Complete the dialogues.

(1)Q：安娜，你还要什么？

A：________________________________。

(2)Q：________________________________

A：一共六十一元。

5. 翻译。

Translate.

(1)今天大卫在街舞比赛中获得了一等奖。

____

(2)这些一共多少钱？

____

(3)我要一大包薯片和一杯奶茶。

____

(4)It's my treat today.

____

(5)To celebrate it, he invites his friends to the convenience store to buy snacks.

____

6. 听写。

Dictation.

ài hào
5. 爱好

dà wèi hé ōu wén yī qǐ qù shè zhāo xīn huì
（大卫和欧文一起去社招新会。）

ōu wén dà wèi nǐ yǒu shén me ài hào ma
欧文：大卫，你有什么爱好吗？

dà wèi wǒ xǐ huan jiē wǔ wǒ xiǎng jiā rù wǔ dǎo shè nǐ ne
大卫：我喜欢街舞，我想加入舞蹈社。你呢？

ōu wén wǒ duì shū fǎ hěn gǎn xìng qù suǒ yǐ wǒ xiǎng jiā rù shū huà shè
欧文：我对书法很感兴趣，所以我想加入书画社。

dà wèi nǐ hái yǒu shén me bié de ài hào ma
大卫：你还有什么别的爱好吗？

ōu wén wǒ xǐ huan kàn shū hé tīng gē
欧文：我喜欢看书和听歌。

dà wèi wǒ yě xǐ huan kàn shū
大卫：我也喜欢看书。

5. Hobbies

(David and Owen go to the association recruitment campaign together.)

Owen: David, what is your hobby?

David: I like street dance. I want to join the dance club. And you?

Owen: I am very interested in calligraphy, so I'd like to join the calligraphy and painting club.

David: Do you have any other hobbies?

Owen: I like reading books and listening to music.

David: I also like reading books.

词汇 (cí huì) Vocabulary

yī qǐ 一起	*adverb*	together
shè tuán 社团	*noun*	association, club
zhāo xīn huì 招新会	*noun*	recruitment campaign
ài hào 爱好	*noun*	hobby
jiē wǔ 街舞	*noun*	street dance
jiā rù 加入	*verb*	join
shū fǎ 书法	*noun*	calligraphy
gǎn xìng qù 感兴趣	*adjective*	interested
huà 画	*noun*	painting
bié de 别的	*adjective*	other
kàn shū 看书	*phrase*	read books
tīng gē 听歌	*phrase*	listen to music

课后习题
Exercises

1. 请在括号里写出对应的拼音或汉字。

Please write down the right syllables or Chinese characters in the parentheses.

兴趣(　　　　)　街舞(　　　　)　看书(　　　　)　听歌(　　　　)

jiā rù(　　　　)　shè tuán(　　　　)　ài hào(　　　　)　yì qǐ(　　　　)

2. 组词。

Combine words.

aì 爱（　　）（　　）	shū 书（　　）（　　）	jiā 加（　　）（　　）	tīng 听（　　）（　　）

3. 用下列所给词语组句。

Complete the sentences with the words given below.

(1)加入　我　舞蹈社　想　你呢　？

____

(2)对　我　书法　感兴趣　很　。

____

(3)还有　你　什么　爱好　别的　吗　？

____

(4)看书　喜欢　听歌　和　我　。

____

4. 完成对话。

Complete the dialogues.

(1)Q：______________________________？

A：我喜欢街舞。

(2) Q：你还有什么别的爱好吗？

A：______________________________。

(3) Q：你想加入什么社团？

A：______________________________。

5. 翻译。

Translate.

(1)大卫，你有什么爱好吗？

____

(2)我想加入舞蹈社，你呢？

____

(3)我对书法很感兴趣。

(4)Do you have any other hobbies?

(5)I like reading books and listening to music.

6. 听写。

Dictation.

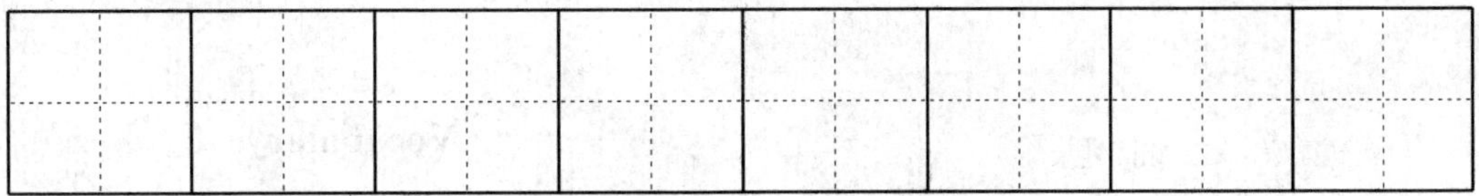

zhí yè guī huà
6. 职 业 规 划

6. Career plans

ōu wén ān nà dà wèi hé hǎi lún zài kè
(欧 文、安 娜、大 卫 和 海 伦 在 课
jiān xián liáo
间 闲 聊。)

(Owen, Anna, David and Helen are chatting at break.)

dà wèi hǎi lún nǐ bì yè yǐ hòu xiǎng zuò
大 卫:海 伦,你 毕 业 以 后 想 做
shén me
什 么?

David: Helen, what do you want to do after graduation?

hǎi lún wǒ xiǎng zuò yī míng xiǎo xué hàn yǔ
海 伦:我 想 做 一 名 小 学 汉 语
lǎo shī yīn wèi wǒ hěn xǐ huan xiǎo hái
老 师。因 为 我 很 喜 欢 小 孩
zi nà nǐ ne
子。那 你 呢?

Helen: I want to be a Chinese teacher in a primary school. Because I like kids very much. What about you?

ōu wén wǒ xiǎng qù cān jūn wǒ jué de chéng
欧 文:我 想 去 参 军,我 觉 得 成
wéi yī míng jūn rén fēi cháng guāng róng ān
为 一 名 军 人 非 常 光 荣。安
nà nǐ ne
娜 你 呢?

Owen: I want to join the army. I think it is very honored to be a soldier. Anna, what about you?

ān nà yǐ qián wǒ xiǎng dāng yī míng yī shēng dàn shì nà tài nán le bì yè yǐ hòu wǒ xiǎng dāng yī míng kuài jì
安娜：以前我想当一名医生，但是那太难了。毕业以后我想当一名会计。

Anna: I wanted to be a doctor before, but that was too hard. After graduation, I want to be an accountant.

dà wèi wǒ xiàn zài zài fǔ xiū fǎ xué bì yè yǐ hòu xiǎng zuò yī míng lǜ shī
大卫：我现在在辅修法学，毕业以后想做一名律师。

David: I'm minoring in law now and I want to be a lawyer after graduation.

cí huì 词汇 Vocabulary

xián liáo 闲聊	*verb* chat
bì yè 毕业	*noun* graduation
yǐ hòu 以后	*preposition* after
xiǎo xué 小学	*noun* primary school
yīn wèi 因为	*conjunction* because
cān jūn 参军	*verb phrase* join the army
jūn rén 军人	*noun* soldier
guāng róng 光荣	*adjective* honored
yǐ qián 以前	*preposition* before
yī shēng 医生	*noun* doctor

nán
难 *adjective* hard

kuài jì
会 计 *noun* accountant

fǔ xiū
辅 修 *verb* minor

fǎ xué
法 学 *noun* law

lǜ shī
律 师 *noun* lawyer

课后习题
Exercises

1. 请在括号里写出对应的拼音或汉字。

Please write down the right syllables or Chinese characters in the parentheses.

闲聊(　　) 毕业(　　) 小学(　　) 因为(　　)

yī shēng(　　) kuài jì(　　) lǜ shī(　　) nán(　　)

2. 组词。

Combine words.

chéng 成 {(　　) (　　)} jūn 军 {(　　) (　　)} cān 参 {(　　) (　　)} guāng 光 {(　　) (　　)}

3. 用下列所给词语组句。

Complete the sentences with the words given below.

(1)毕业 你 以后 什么 做 想 ?

____

(2)一名 我 小学 做 老师 想 汉语 。

____

(3)医生 以前 我 一名 做 想 。

____

(4)我　光荣　成为　觉得　一名　非常　军人　。

____

4. 完成对话。

Complete the dialogues.

(1)Q：____？

A：我想做一名小学汉语老师。

(2)Q：你为什么想去参军？

A：____。

(3)Q：你在辅修法学吗？

A：____。

5. 翻译。

Translate.

(1)海伦，你毕业以后想做什么？

____

(2)我想做一名小学汉语老师。

____

(3)因为我很喜欢小孩子。

____

(4)I want to join the army.

____

(5)After graduation，I want to be an accountant.

____

6. 听写

Dictation.

jiā tíng chéng yuán

7. 家庭成员

ān nà hé hǎi lún zài sù shè liáo dào le zì jǐ de jiā rén

（安娜和海伦在宿舍聊到了自己的家人。）

hǎi lún nǐ jiā lǐ yǒu jǐ gè rén

海伦：你家里有几个人？

ān nà wǔ gè wǒ de yé ye nǎi nai bà ba mā ma hé wǒ

安娜：五个。我的爷爷、奶奶、爸爸、妈妈和我。

wǒ bà ba shì wài kē yī shēng wǒ mā ma shì jiā tíng zhǔ fù nǐ jiā ne

我爸爸是外科医生，我妈妈是家庭主妇。你家呢？

hǎi lún wǒ jiā lǐ yǒu sì kǒu rén bà ba mā ma wǒ hái yǒu yī gè shí suì de dì di

海伦：我家里有四口人。爸爸、妈妈、我，还有一个十岁的弟弟。

wǒ bà ba mā ma dōu shì lǎo shī wǒ dì di zài dú xiǎo xué wǔ nián jí

我爸爸妈妈都是老师，我弟弟在读小学五年级。

ān nà wa nǐ dì di shì bu shì hěn kě ài

安娜：哇，你弟弟是不是很可爱？

hǎi lún shì dàn tā hěn tiáo pí

海伦：是，但他很调皮。

7. Family members

(Anna and Helen are talking about their family members in the dormitory.)

Helen: How many people are there in your family?

Anna: Five. My grandfather, grandmother, Dad, Mom and me.

My father is a surgeon and my mother is a housewife. How about your family?

Helen: There are four members in my family. Dad, Mom, me and a younger brother who is ten years old.

My parents are both teachers, and my younger brother is in the fifth grade of primary school.

Anna: Wow, is your brother very lovely?

Helen: Yes, but he is very naughty.

词汇 cí huì　　Vocabulary

家人 jiā rén	*noun*	family member
爷爷 yé ye	*noun*	grandfather
奶奶 nǎi nai	*noun*	grandmother
爸爸 bà ba	*noun*	father，dad
妈妈 mā ma	*noun*	mother，mom
父母 fù mǔ	*noun*	parents
外科医生 wài kē yī shēng	*noun*	surgeon
家庭主妇 jiā tíng zhǔ fù	*noun*	housewife
弟弟 dì di	*noun*	younger brother
可爱 kě ài	*adjective*	lovely
调皮 tiáo pí	*adjective*	naughty

课后习题
Exercises

1. 请在括号里写出对应的拼音或汉字。

Please write down the right syllables or Chinese characters in the parentheses.

家人(　　　)　父母(　　　)　外科(　　　)　家庭(　　　)

lǎo shī(　　　)　dì di(　　　)　kě ài(　　　)　tiáo pí(　　　)

2. 组词。

Combine words.

jiā 家 ( ) ( )　　tiáo 调 ( ) ( )　　zhǔ 主 ( ) ( )　　liáo 聊 ( ) ( )

3. 用下列所给词语组句。

Complete the sentences with the words given below.

(1)几个人　你　有　家里　？

______

(2)爸爸　我　是　医生　外科　。

______

(3)弟弟　我　五年级　在读　小学　。

______

4. 完成对话。

Complete the dialogues.

(1)Q：______？

A：五个。我的爷爷、奶奶、爸爸、妈妈和我。

(2)Q：你弟弟是不是很可爱？

A：______。

(3)Q：海伦，你爸爸妈妈是做什么的？

A：______。

5. 翻译。

Translate.

(1)你家里有几个人？

______

(2)我妈妈是家庭主妇。

______

(3) My younger brother is in the fifth grade of primary school.

______

(4) Yes, but he is very naughty.

---

6. 听写

Dictation.

8. 时间 (shí jiān)

8. Time

jīn tiān shì zhōu liù ōu wén hé dà wèi zài sù shè shuì jiào zhè shí ōu wén de nào zhōng xiǎng le
(今天是周六，欧文和大卫在宿舍睡觉，这时欧文的闹钟响了。)

(Today is Saturday. Owen and David are sleeping in the dormitory. At this time, Owen's alarm clock is ringing.)

dà wèi xiàn zài jǐ diǎn le
大卫：现在几点了？

David: What time is it now?

ōu wén jiǔ diǎn chà yī kè
欧文：九点差一刻。

Owen: It is a quarter to nine.

dà wèi tiān na wǒ gāi qǐ chuáng le wǒ jiǔ diǎn bàn yǒu yī gè wǔ dǎo shè de huó dòng
大卫：天哪，我该起床了。我九点半有一个舞蹈社的活动。

David: Oh, my God. I should get up. I have a dance club activity at 9:30.

ōu wén nà nǐ kuài diǎn qǐ lái ba bié wàng le chī zǎo cān
欧文：那你快点起来吧！别忘了吃早餐。

Owen: Get up quickly! Do not forget to eat breakfast.

dà wèi nǐ jīn tiān méi yǒu ān pái ma
大卫：你今天没有安排吗？

David: Don't you have any plans today?

ōu wén yǒu a wǒ jì huà shí diǎn guò wǔ fēn hé ān nà yī qǐ qù tú shū guǎn xué xí
欧文：有啊。我计划十点过五分和安娜一起去图书馆学习。

Owen：Yes. I plan to go to the library with Anna to study at five past ten.

cí huì 词汇 — Vocabulary

shuì jiào 睡觉	*verb* sleep
nào zhōng 闹钟	*noun* alarm clock
xiǎng 响	*verb* ring
yī kè 一刻	*noun* a quarter；one quarter
qǐ chuáng 起床	*verb* get up
huó dòng 活动	*noun* activity
kuài diǎn 快点	*adverb* quickly
zǎo cān 早餐	*noun* breakfast
ān pái 安排	*verb* plan
tú shū guǎn 图书馆	*noun* library
xué xí 学习	*verb* study

课后习题
Exercises

1. 请在括号里写出对应的拼音或汉字。

Please write down the right syllables or Chinese characters in the parentheses.

睡觉（　　　）　闹钟（　　　）　一刻（　　　）　起床（　　　）

huó dòng（　　　）　xué xí（　　　）

xiǎng（　　　）　tú shū guǎn（　　　）

2. 组词。

Combine words.

xiǎng 响 {（　　）（　　）　huó 活 {（　　）（　　）　ān 安 {（　　）（　　）　xué 学 {（　　）（　　）

3. 用下列所给词语组句。

Complete the sentences with the words given below.

(1)几点　现在　了　？

____

(2)九点半　舞蹈社　我　有　活动　一个　的　。

____

(3)忘了　早餐　吃　别　。

____

(4)安排　你　今天　吗　没有　？

____

4. 完成对话。

Complete the dialogues.

(1)Q：______________________________？

A：九点差一刻。

(2)Q：你今天没有安排吗？

A：____。

(3)Q：大卫，你有什么事吗？

A：____。

5. 翻译。

Translate.

(1)别忘了吃早餐。

____

(2)我九点半有一个舞蹈社的活动。

____

(3)你今天没有安排吗？

____

(4)What time is it now?

____

(5)It's a quarter to nine.

____

6. 听写

Dictation.

9. 假期 (jià qī)

9. Holiday

(五一快到了，同学们在讨论如何度过这个假期。)
(wǔ yī kuài dào le, tóng xué men zài tǎo lùn rú hé dù guò zhè ge jià qī.)

(May Day is coming. The students are discussing how to spend the holiday.)

hǎi lún wǒ zhǔn bèi huí jiā wǒ xiǎng chī wǒ
海伦：我准备回家，我想吃我
mā ma zuò de cài le nǐ men ne
妈妈做的菜了。你们呢？

Helen: I am going home. I want to eat the dishes my mom cooks. What about you?

ōu wén hǎo xiàn mù nǐ néng huí jiā wǒ yě
欧文：好羡慕你能回家。我也
xiǎng huí jiā dàn shì wǒ jiā tài yuǎn le
想回家，但是我家太远了。
zuì jìn xiǎng mǎi yī shuāng xié zi wǒ zhǔn
最近想买一双鞋子，我准
bèi qù zhǎo yī gè jiān zhí zhuàn diǎn líng
备去找一个兼职，赚点零
huā qián
花钱。

Owen: I envy you for going home. I want to go home, too. But it is too far away. Recently I want to buy a pair of shoes so I am going to find a part-time job to earn some pocket money.

ān nà wǒ zhǔn bèi hé wǒ de péng you chū
安娜：我准备和我的朋友出
qù wán wǔ hàn hái yǒu hěn duō dì fāng wǒ
去玩。武汉还有很多地方我
méi qù guò bǐ rú huáng hè lóu hé cháng
没去过，比如，黄鹤楼和长
jiāng dà qiáo
江大桥。

Anna: I plan to go out with my friends. There are many places in Wuhan that I have not visited, such as the Yellow Crane Tower and the Yangtze River Bridge.

dà wèi mǎ shàng jiù yào kǎo shì le wǒ zhǔn
大卫：马上就要考试了，我准
bèi liú zài xué xiào fù xí
备留在学校复习。

David: The exam is coming soon. I am going to stay at school to review.

cí huì 词汇 / Vocabulary

dù guò
度过 — *verb* spend

jià qī
假期 — *noun* holiday

xiàn mù
羡慕 — *verb* envy

zuì jìn 最近	*adverb* recently
xié zi 鞋子	*noun* shoes
jiān zhí 兼职	*noun* part-time job
zhuàn 赚	*verb* earn
líng huā qián 零花钱	*noun* pocket money
kǎo shì 考试	*noun* exam
fù xí 复习	*verb* review

课后习题
Exercises

1. 请在括号里写出对应的拼音或汉字。

Please write down the right syllables or Chinese characters in the parentheses.

度过（ ） 假期（ ） 羡慕（ ） 最近（ ）

jiān zhí（ ） zhuàn（ ） kǎo shì（ ） fù xí（ ）

2. 组词。

Combine words.

kǎo 考{（ ）（ ） dù 度{（ ）（ ） fù 复{（ ）（ ） qī 期{（ ）（ ）

3. 用下列所给词语组句。

Complete the sentences with the words given below.

（1）妈妈 我 菜 想 做 的 吃 我 了 。

____

(2)我　但是　家　远　太　了　。

____

(3)准备　和　玩　出去　我　朋友　我的　一起　。

____

(4)考试　马上　就要　了　。

____

4. 完成对话。

Complete the dialogues.

(1)Q：______________________________？

A：五一我准备回家。

(2)Q：欧文，你不能回家吗？

A：______________________________。

(3)Q：安娜，你五一准备干什么？

A：______________________________。

5. 翻译。

Translate.

(1)同学们在讨论如何度过这个假期。

____

(2)武汉还有很多地方我没有去过。

____

(3)我准备留在学校复习。

____

(4)I want to go home, too. But it is too far away.

____

(5)The exam is coming soon.

____

6. 听写

Dictation.

10. 运动会

yùn dòng huì

10. The sports meeting

yī nián yī dù de xiào yuán yùn dòng huì jiù yào kāi shǐ le, dà jiā dōu zài kǎo lǜ bào míng cān jiā nǎ gè xiàng mù.

（一年一度的校园运动会就要开始了，大家都在考虑报名参加哪个项目。）

(The annual campus sports meeting is about to begin, and everyone is considering which project to sign up for.)

hǎi lún: yùn dòng huì yào lái le, nǐ men dōu bào míng le shén me xiàng mù?

海伦：运动会要来了，你们都报名了什么项目？

Helen: The sports meeting is coming. What projects do you sign up for?

dà wèi: wǒ bào míng le nán zǐ yī qiān mǐ cháng pǎo hé tiào yuǎn. zhè shì wǒ shàn cháng de tǐ yù xiàng mù, wǒ yǒu xìn xīn ná dào míng cì. nǐ men ne?

大卫：我报名了男子一千米长跑和跳远。这是我擅长的体育项目，我有信心拿到名次。你们呢？

David: I signed up for the men's one-kilometer long-distance run and long jump. I am good at these sports. So, I am confident of winning a place. What about you?

ān nà: wǒ bào le qiān qiú hé nǚ zǐ wǔ shí mǐ duǎn pǎo. zhè xiē xiàng mù shì bǐ jiào jiǎn dān de. zhòng zài cān yù.

安娜：我报了铅球和女子五十米短跑。这些项目是比较简单的。重在参与。

Anna: I signed up for shot put and women's 50-meter sprint. These projects are easier. Participation is vital.

ōu wén wǒ jué de nà ge zhì chuān hū lā
欧文：我觉得那个智穿呼啦
quān de tuán tǐ xiàng mù hěn yǒu qù, wǒ men
圈的团体项目很有趣，我们
yī qǐ qù cān jiā ba
一起去参加吧！

Owen: I think the group project, going through hula hoops with strategies, is very interesting. Let's sign up for it together.

cí huì
词汇 Vocabulary

yī nián yī dù de 一年一度的	*adjective* annual
yùn dòng huì 运动会	*noun* sports meeting
kǎo lǜ 考虑	*verb* consider
bào míng 报名	*verb* sign up
xiàng mù 项目	*noun* project
cháng pǎo 长跑	*noun* long-distance run
tiào yuǎn 跳远	*noun* long jump
shàn cháng 擅长	*verb* be good at
qiān qiú 铅球	*noun* shot
duǎn pǎo 短跑	*noun* sprint
cān yù 参与	*noun* participation
tuán tǐ 团体	*noun* group

课后习题
Exercises

1. 请在括号里写出对应的拼音或汉字。

Please write down the right syllables or Chinese characters in the parentheses.

考虑(　　　)　　擅长(　　　)　　项目(　　　)　　长跑(　　　)

yì nián yí dù(　　　)　　bào míng(　　　)

cān yù(　　　)　　tuán tǐ(　　　)

2. 组词。

Combine words.

bào 报 {(　　) (　　)}　　tuán 团 {(　　) (　　)}　　tiào 跳 {(　　) (　　)}　　bǐ 比 {(　　) (　　)}

3. 用下列所给词语组句。

Complete the sentences with the words given below.

(1)校园　一年一度的　要　运动会　开始　了　。

____

(2)你们　项目　参加　都　了　什么　？

____

(3)这个　我　体育　擅长　项目　。

____

(4)短跑　简单　是　比较　的　项目　体育　。

____

4. 完成对话。

Complete the dialogues.

(1)Q：安娜，你想赢得比赛吗？

A：______________________________。

(2)Q：____?

A:我报了铅球和女子五十米短跑。

(3)Q：大卫,你为什么报名参加了长跑?

A:____。

5.翻译。

Translate.

(1)一年一度的校园运动会就要开始了。

____

(2)大家都在考虑报名参加哪个项目。

____

(3)我擅长跑步。

____

(4)I am confident of winning a place.

____

(5)I think the group project is very interesting.

____

6.听写

Dictation.

11.水果 (shuǐ guǒ)

11. Fruits

(海伦和安娜一起去买水果。)
hǎi lún hé ān nà yī qǐ qù mǎi shuǐ guǒ

(Helen and Anna go to buy fruits together.)

安娜:海伦你看,好多新鲜的水果啊!
ān nà hǎi lún nǐ kàn hǎo duō xīn xiān de shuǐ guǒ a

Anna: Helen. Look, there are so many fresh fruits!

hǎi lún duì a wǒ zhǔn bèi duō mǎi jǐ zhǒng shuǐ guǒ píng guǒ lí zi táo zi hé yīng táo wǒ dōu ài chī

海伦：对啊。我准备多买几种水果。苹果、梨子、桃子和樱桃我都爱吃。

Helen: That's right. I am going to buy several more kinds of fruits. I like eating apples, pears, peaches and cherries.

ān nà wǒ zhǔn bèi mǎi jǐ gè máng guǒ zài mǎi yī xiǎo kuài liú lián kě xī xiàn zài méi yǒu xī guā wǒ zuì ài chī xī guā le

安娜：我准备买几个芒果，再买一小块榴莲。可惜现在没有西瓜，我最爱吃西瓜了。

Anna: I am going to buy some mangoes and a small piece of durian. Unfortunately, watermelons are not available now. I like them best.

diàn yuán zhè shì gāng dào de lì zhī fēi cháng xīn xiān yào bu yào lái yī diǎn

店员：这是刚到的荔枝，非常新鲜，要不要来一点？

Clerk: These are the litchis which just arrived recently. They are very fresh. Would you like some?

hǎi lún bù yòng le xiè xie wǒ bù ài chī lì zhī ér qiě wǒ yǐ jīng mǎi le hěn duō le

海伦：不用了，谢谢，我不爱吃荔枝，而且我已经买了很多了。

Helen: No, thanks. I don't like litchis, and I've already bought a lot.

cí huì 词汇 / Vocabulary

shuǐ guǒ 水果	*noun* fruit
xīn xiān de 新鲜的	*adjective* fresh
píng guǒ 苹果	*noun* apple
lí zi 梨子	*noun* pear

táo zi 桃子	*noun*	peach
yīng táo 樱桃	*noun*	cherry
máng guǒ 芒果	*noun*	mango
liú lián 榴莲	*noun*	durian
xī guā 西瓜	*noun*	watermelon
lì zhī 荔枝	*noun*	litchi

课后习题
Exercises

1. 请在括号里写出对应的拼音或汉字。

Please write down the right syllables or Chinese characters in the parentheses.

水果(　　　)　新鲜(　　　)　苹果(　　　)　樱桃(　　　)

xī guā(　　　)　máng guǒ(　　　)lí zi(　　　)　táo zi(　　　)

2. 组词。

Combine words.

shuǐ 水 {(　　) (　　)}　xīn 新 {(　　) (　　)}　mǎi 买 {(　　) (　　)}　zuì 最 {(　　) (　　)}

3. 用下列所给词语组句。

Complete the sentences with the words given below.

(1)新鲜　的　水果　好多　。

____

(2)现在　可惜　西瓜　没有　。

____

(3)刚到的　这　荔枝　是　。

____

(4)很多　已经　我　了　买了　。

____

4. 完成对话。

Complete the dialogues.

(1)Q：安娜，你最爱吃什么水果？

A：______________________________。

(2)Q：安娜，你买西瓜了吗？

A：______________________________。

(3)Q：要不要买一点荔枝？

A：______________________________。

5. 翻译。

Translate.

(1)海伦你看，好多新鲜的水果啊！

____

(2)这是刚到的荔枝。

____

(3)我已经买了很多了。

____

(4)What's your favorite fruit?

____

(5)Unfortunately，watermelons are not available now.

____

6. 听写

Dictation.

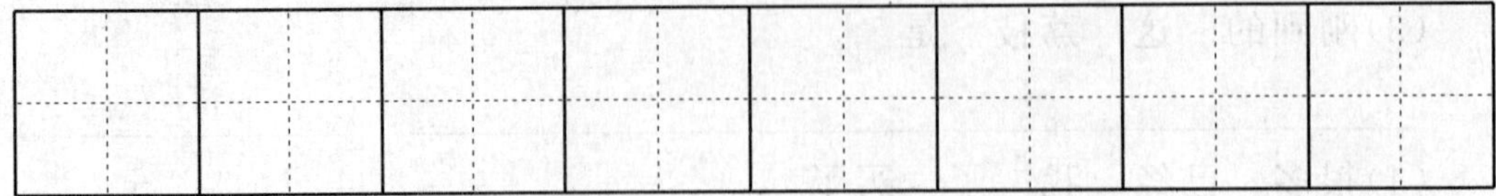

12. 住酒店（zhù jiǔ diàn）

12. Checking in at the hotel

ōu wén dà wèi ān nà hé hǎi lún jié bàn chū yóu rù zhù jiǔ diàn
（欧文、大卫、安娜和海伦结伴出游，入住酒店。）

(Owen, David, Anna and Helen travel together, and check in at the hotel.)

qián tái huān yíng guāng lín
前台：欢迎光临！

Receptionist: Welcome!

ōu wén nǐ hǎo qǐng wèn hái yǒu fáng jiān ma
欧文：你好，请问还有房间吗？

Owen: Hello, is there any room available?

qián tái yǒu de dān jiān biāo jiān dōu hái yǒu dān jiān shì yuán yī wǎn biāo jiān shì yuán yī wǎn
前台：有的，单间、标间都还有。单间是150元一晚，标间是200元一晚。

Receptionist: Yes, there are both standard rooms and single rooms. The single room is 150 yuan a night and the standard room is 200 yuan a night.

dà wèi wǒ men xū yào liǎng gè biāo jiān zhù yī gè wǎn shang
大卫：我们需要两个标间，住一个晚上。

David: We need two standard rooms for one night.

qián tái hǎo de qǐng chū shì yī xià nǐ men de zhèng jiàn wǒ dēng jì yī xià
前台：好的，请出示一下你们的证件，我登记一下。

Receptionist: OK. Please show me your certificates and I'll register you.

ān nà zhè shì wǒ men de hù zhào
安娜：这是我们的护照。

Anna: These are our passports.

qián tái zhè shì nǐ men de fáng kǎ qǐng yú
前台：这是你们的房卡，请于
míng tiān zhōng wǔ shí èr diǎn qián tuì fáng
明天中午十二点前退房。
rú guǒ yǒu rèn hé xū yào qǐng bō dǎ qián
如果有任何需要，请拨打前
tái diàn huà
台电话。

Receptionist: Here are your room cards. Please check out before 12:00 a. m. tomorrow. If you need anything, please call the front desk.

hǎi lún hǎo de xiè xie
海伦：好的，谢谢。

Helen: OK, thank you.

cí huì
词汇

Vocabulary

chū yóu
出游 *verb* travel

jiǔ diàn
酒店 *noun* hotel

fáng jiān
房间 *noun* room

dān jiān
单间 *noun* single room

biāo jiān
标间 *noun* standard room

chū shì
出示 *verb* show

hù zhào
护照 *noun* passport

dēng jì
登记 *verb* register

tuì fáng
退房 *phrase* check out

xū yào
需要 *verb* need

课后习题
Exercises

1. 请在括号里写出对应的拼音或汉字。

Please write down the right syllables or Chinese characters in the parentheses.

出游（　　） 酒店（　　） 房间（　　） 护照（　　）

qián tái（　　） chū shì（　　） dēng jì（　　） xū yào（　　）

2. 组词。

Combine words.

chū 出 {（　　）（　　）　dēng 登 {（　　）（　　）　tùi 退 {（　　）（　　）　xū 需 {（　　）（　　）

3. 用下列所给词语组句。

Complete the sentences with the words given below.

(1)房间　你好　请问　吗　还有　？

____

(2)单间　还有　标间　都　。

____

(3)出示　请　的　护照　你们　。

____

(4)十二点　请　中午　于　退房　前　明天　。

____

4. 完成对话。

Complete the dialogues.

(1)Q：______________________________？

A：有的，单间标间都有。

(2)Q：你们要什么房间？住多久？

A：______________________________。

(3)Q：____？

A：请于明天中午十二点前退房。

5. 翻译。

Translate.

(1)请问还有房间吗？

____

(2)如果有任何需要，请拨打前台电话。

____

(3)请于明天中午十二点前退房。

____

(4)We need two standard rooms for one night.

____

(5)Please show me your passports and I will register for you.

____

6. 听写

Dictation.

13. 请假 (qǐng jià)

13. Asking for leave

(大卫在社团活动中扭伤了脚，于是他打电话向王老师请假。)

(dà wèi zài shè tuán huó dòng zhōng niǔ shāng le jiǎo, yú shì tā dǎ diàn huà xiàng wáng lǎo shī qǐng jià.)

(David sprained his foot in the club activity. So, he makes a phone call to Mr. Wang for leave.)

dà wèi wèi nín hǎo qǐng wèn shì wáng lǎo shī ma
大卫：喂，您好，请问是王老师吗？

David: Hello, is that Mr. Wang?

wáng lǎo shī shì de
王老师：是的。

Mr. Wang: Yes.

dà wèi wǒ shì hàn yǔ zhuān yè yī bān de dà wèi zuó tiān wǒ cān jiā shè tuán huó dòng shí bù xiǎo xīn niǔ shāng le jiǎo xiǎng xiàng nín qǐng yī tiān jià zài sù shè xiū xi hái xī wàng nín néng pī zhǔn
大卫：我是汉语专业一班的大卫。昨天我参加社团活动时，不小心扭伤了脚。想向您请一天假在宿舍休息。还希望您能批准。

David: I'm David from the Chinese major Class One. I carelessly sprained my foot when I was joining in the club activity yesterday. So, I would like to ask you for a day off to rest in the dormitory. I hope you can approve it.

wáng lǎo shī hǎo de wǒ zhī dào le nǐ zài sù shè hǎo hǎo xiū xi
王老师：好的，我知道了，你在宿舍好好休息。

Mr. Wang: OK, I see. Take a good rest in the dormitory.

dà wèi hǎo de xiè xie lǎo shī
大卫：好的，谢谢老师。

David: OK, thank you very much.

cí huì
词汇

Vocabulary

niǔ shāng
扭伤 — *verb* sprain

diàn huà
电话 — *noun* phone

qǐng jià
请假 — *phrase* ask for leave

zuó tiān
昨天 — *noun* yesterday

bù xiǎo xīn 不小心	*adverb* carelessly
pī zhǔn 批准	*verb* approve
sù shè 宿舍	*noun* dormitory
xī wàng 希望	*verb* hope

课后习题
Exercises

1. 请在括号里写出对应的拼音或汉字。

Please write down the right syllables or Chinese characters in the parentheses.

扭伤(　　　)　电话(　　　)　请假(　　　)　昨天(　　　)

bù xiǎo xīn(　　　)　xī wàng(　　　)

pī zhǔn(　　　)　sù shè(　　　)

2. 组词。

Combine words.

niǔ 扭 {(　　) (　　)}　dǎ 打 {(　　) (　　)}　shè 社 {(　　) (　　)}　pī 批 {(　　) (　　)}

3. 用下列所给词语组句。

Complete the sentences with the words given below.

(1)王老师　请问　吗　是　?

____

(2)扭伤　昨天　脚　参加　我　活动　了　社团　不小心　时　。

____

(3)请假 您 想 休息 向 宿舍 在 。

____

(4)您 批准 能 希望 。

____

4. 完成对话。

Complete the dialogues.

(1)Q:____?

A:是的。

(2)Q:你为什么要请假?

A:____。

(3)Q:____?

A:想向您请一天假。

5. 翻译。

Translate.

(1)我打电话向王老师请假。

____

(2)我不小心扭伤了脚。

____

(3) I carelessly sprained my foot when I joined in the club activity yesterday.

____

(4)I would like to ask you for a day off to rest in the dormitory.

____

6. 听写

Dictation.

gōng jiāo zhī fù
14. 公交支付

dà wèi hé ōu wén chū mén zhǔn bèi chéng gōng jiāo ōu wén fā xiàn zì jǐ wàng le dài gōng jiāo kǎ
(大卫和欧文出门,准备乘公交。欧文发现自己忘了带公交卡。)

ōu wén zāo le wǒ wàng jì dài gōng jiāo kǎ le děng huì er nǐ néng bāng wǒ shuā kǎ ma
欧文:糟了,我忘记带公交卡了,等会儿你能帮我刷卡吗?

dà wèi wǒ zǎo jiù bù yòng gōng jiāo kǎ le wǒ xiàn zài yī zhí dōu zài yòng zhī fù bǎo zhī fù bǎo shàng de diàn zǐ gōng jiāo kǎ bù jǐn hěn fāng biàn ér qiě hái hěn yōu huì
大卫:我早就不用公交卡了。我现在一直都在用支付宝。支付宝上的电子公交卡不仅很方便而且还很优惠。

ōu wén à wǒ míng bái le wǒ yī zhí wàng le kāi tōng chèn gōng jiāo hái méi lái wǒ kāi tōng yī xià
欧文:啊,我明白了。我一直忘了开通。趁公交还没来,我开通一下。

dà wèi xiàn zài yí dòng zhī fù kě fāng biàn le zhǐ yào yǒu shǒu jī méi shén me shì bàn bù dào
大卫:现在移动支付可方便了。只要有手机,没什么事办不到。

14. Bus payment

(David and Owen go out and plan to take the bus. Owen finds that he forgets to bring his bus card.)

Owen: Oops, I forget to bring my bus card. Could you help me swipe the card later?

David: I haven't used my bus card for a long time. I use Alipay all the time. The electronic bus card in Alipay is not only very convenient but also very concessional.

Owen: Ah, I see. I forgot to add it to my Alipay. I'll add it before the bus comes.

David: Now mobile payment is very convenient. As long as you have a smart phone, nothing is impossible.

词汇 (cí huì) Vocabulary

发现 (fā xiàn)	*verb* find
忘记 (wàng jì)	*verb* forget
公交卡 (gōng jiāo kǎ)	*noun* bus card, bus pass
支付宝 (zhī fù bǎo)	*noun* Alipay
电子 (diàn zǐ)	*adjective* electronic
不仅……而且 (bù jǐn……ér qiě)	*phrase* not only... but also...
优惠的 (yōu huì de)	*adjective* concessional
开通 (kāi tōng)	*verb* add
支付 (zhī fù)	*noun* payment
手机 (shǒu jī)	*noun* mobile phone, cell phone
移动支付 (yí dòng zhī fù)	*noun* mobile payment

课后习题

Exercises

1. 请在括号里写出对应的拼音或汉字。

Please write down the right syllables or Chinese characters in the parentheses.

忘记(　　　)　发现(　　　)　支付(　　　)　电子(　　　)

bù jǐn(　　　)　ér qiě(　　　)　kāi tōng(　　　)　shǒu jī(　　　)

2. 组词。

Combine words.

chéng 乘 ( ) ( )	dài 带 ( ) ( )	bāng 帮 ( ) ( )	yí 移 ( ) ( )

3. 用下列所给词语组句。

Complete the sentences with the words given below.

(1)欧文　公交卡　发现　忘了　自己　带　。

____

(2)不仅　电子公交卡　很　而且　方便　很　优惠　。

____

(3)公交　没来　趁　赶快　我　它　开通　。

____

(4)有了　办不到　手机　什么事　没　。

____

4. 完成对话。

Complete the dialogues.

(1)Q：欧文，你怎么了？

A：______________________________。

(2)Q：你不用公交卡的话用的是什么？

A：______________________________。

5. 翻译。

Translate.

(1)欧文发现自己忘了带公交卡。

____

(2)支付宝上的电子公交卡不仅很方便而且很优惠。

____

(3)As long as you have a smart phone, nothing is impossible.

____

(4)I haven't used my bus card for a long time.

____

6. 听写

Dictation.

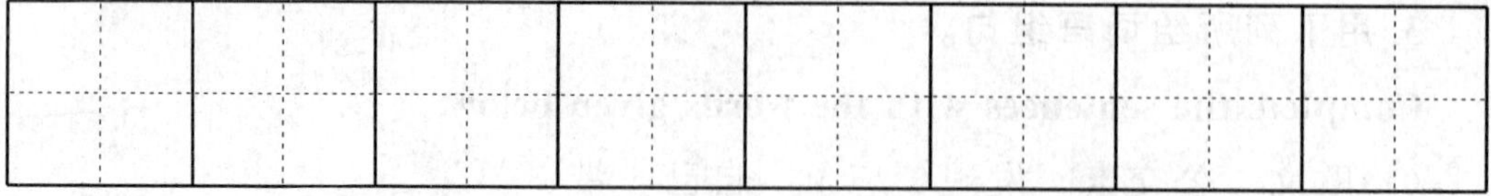

jiǎn féi
15. 减 肥

xià tiān kuài dào le wèi le chuān shàng hǎo kàn de duǎn qún ān nà hé hǎi lún jué dìng jiǎn féi
(夏天快到了,为了穿上好看的短裙,安娜和海伦决定减肥。)

ān nà xià tiān kuài dào le wèi le chuān shàng hǎo kàn de duǎn qún wǒ men yī dìng yào shòu
安娜:夏天快到了,为了穿上好看的短裙,我们一定要瘦。

hǎi lún jiǎn féi zhēn de shì yī jiàn hěn kùn nán de shì wǒ bù zhī dào gāi zěn me zuò
海伦:减肥真的是一件很困难的事,我不知道该怎么做。

ān nà jié shí dàn shì zhè yàng hǎo xiàng bù tài jiàn kāng
安娜:节食?但是这样好像不太健康。

hǎi lún dāng rán bù néng la jié shí duì shēn tǐ yǒu shāng hài wǒ men yīng gāi hé lǐ yǐn shí wài jiā shì liàng yùn dòng zuì zhòng yào de shì jiān chí yī dìng bù néng fàng qì
海伦:当然不能啦,节食对身体有伤害。我们应该合理饮食,外加适量运动。最重要的是坚持,一定不能放弃。

15. Losing weight

(Summer is coming. In order to wear beautiful skirts, Anna and Helen decide to lose weight.)

Anna: Summer is coming. In order to wear beautiful skirts, we must be thin enough.

Helen: Losing weight is really a hard thing. I don't know how to do that.

Anna: Go on a diet? But it seems not very healthy.

Helen: Of course not. Diet is harmful to our body. We should have a balanced diet, and appropriate exercise. The most important thing is to stick to it and never give up.

ān nà nà wǒ men měi tiān wǎn shang qù màn pǎo sì shí fēn zhōng 安娜：那我们每天晚上去慢跑四十分钟。	Anna: Let's go jogging for forty minutes every evening.
hǎi lún hǎo nà wǒ men liǎ hù xiāng gǔ lì 海伦：好，那我们俩互相鼓励。	Helen: OK, let's encourage each other.

cí huì
词汇 — Vocabulary

jiǎn féi 减肥	*phrase* lose weight
shòu 瘦	*adjective* thin
kùn nán 困难	*adjective* hard
jié shí 节食	*phrase* be on a diet
hǎo xiàng 好像	*verb* seem
jiàn kāng 健康	*adjective* healthy
shāng hài 伤害	*adjective* harmful
shì liàng 适量	*adjective* appropriate, moderate
jiān chí 坚持	*verb* stick to
fàng qì 放弃	*verb* give up
màn pǎo 慢跑	*verb* jog

课后习题
Exercises

1. 请在括号里写出对应的拼音或汉字。

Please write down the right syllables or Chinese characters in the parentheses.

减肥（　　　　）　瘦（　　　　）　节食（　　　　）　健康（　　　　）

shāng hài（　　　　）　shēn tǐ（　　　　）jiān chí（　　　　）　fàng qì（　　　　）

2. 组词。

Combine words.

jiǎn 减 {（　　） （　　）　　jié 节 {（　　） （　　）　　shāng 伤 {（　　） （　　）　　fàng 放 {（　　） （　　）

3. 用下列所给词语组句。

Complete the sentences with the words given below.

(1)困难　减肥　的　是　事　一件　。

____

(2)我　做　不知道　怎么　该　。

____

(3)伤害　对　节食　身体　有　。

____

(4)合理　应该　我们　饮食　。

____

4. 完成对话。

Complete the dialogues.

(1)Q：为了穿上好看的裙子，我们该怎么办？

A：______________________________。

(2)Q：______________________________？

A：最重要的是坚持。

(3)Q：节食怎么样？

A：____。

5. 翻译。

Translate.

(1)这样好像不太健康。

____

(2)节食对身体有伤害。

____

(3)我们应该合理饮食，外加适量运动。

____

(4)It's really hard to lose weight.

____

(5)The most important thing is to stick to it and never give up.

____

6. 听写

Dictation.

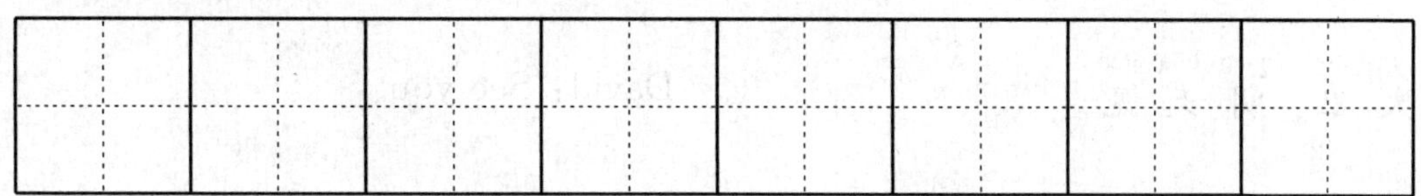

16. 天气 (tiān qì)

16. Weather

dà wèi zǎo shàng hǎo 大卫：早上好。	David：Good morning.
ōu wén zǎo shàng hǎo 欧文：早上好。	Owen：Good morning.
dà wèi nǐ jué de jīn tiān tiān qì zěn me yàng 大卫：你觉得今天天气怎么样？	David：What do you think of the weather today?

ōu wén hěn nuǎn huo 欧文：很暖和。	Owen：It's warm.
dà wèi míng tiān ne 大卫：明天呢？	David：What about tomorrow?
ōu wén tiān qì yù bào shuō míng tiān xià yǔ 欧文：天气预报说明天下雨。	Owen：The weather forecast says it will rain tomorrow.
dà wèi nǐ míng tiān wǎn shang xiǎng zuò shén me 大卫：你明天晚上想做什么？	David：What would you like to do tomorrow evening?
ōu wén hái bù zhī dào，nǐ dǎ suàn zuò shén me 欧文：还不知道，你打算做什么？	Owen：I don't know yet. What are you going to do?
dà wèi nà wǒ men míng tiān qù fàn guǎn ba 大卫：那我们明天去饭馆吧！	David：Let's go to a restaurant tomorrow.
ōu wén hǎo ya，nà míng tiān jiàn 欧文：好呀，那明天见。	Owen：OK，see you tomorrow.
dà wèi míng tiān jiàn 大卫：明天见。	David：See you.

cí huì 词汇　　Vocabulary

tiān qì 天气	*noun* weather
zǎo shàng 早上	*noun* morning
jīn tiān 今天	*noun* today
nuǎn huo 暖和	*adjective* warm

míng tiān
明 天 *noun* tomorrow

xià yǔ
下 雨 *verb* rain

wǎn shang
晚 上 *noun* evening

fàn guǎn
饭 馆 *noun* restaurant

课后习题
Exercises

1. 根据拼音写出汉字。

Write the corresponding Chinese characters according to the syllables.

tiān qì (　　　　) zǎo shàng(　　　　)

jīn tiān(　　　　) nuǎn huo(　　　　)

2. 用所给词语造句。

Make sentences according to the given words.

(1)天气

____

(2)明天

____

(3)饭馆

____

3. 根据课文完成句子。

Fill in the sentences according to the text.

(1)你(　　　)做什么?

(2)那我们(　　　)去饭馆吧。

4. 英译汉。

English-Chinese Translation.

(1) What do you think of the weather today?

____

(2) See you tomorrow.

____

5. 将下列词语组成句子。

Make sentences with the following words.

(1)天气　觉得　你　怎么样

____

(2)打算　你　什么　做

____

6. 听写

Dictation.

17. 如何去黄鹤楼 (rú hé qù huáng hè lóu)

17. How to get to the Yellow Crane Tower

hǎi lún　dǎ rǎo yī xià　qǐng wèn nǐ zhī dào zěn me qù huáng hè lóu ma

海伦：打扰一下。请问你知道怎么去黄鹤楼吗？

Helen: Excuse me. Do you know the way to the Yellow Crane Tower?

ān nà　nǐ kě yǐ chéng zuò 703 lù gōng jiāo, dà gài wǔ shí fēn zhōng jiù néng dào

安娜：你可以乘坐703路公交，大概五十分钟就能到。

Anna: You can take the bus No. 703. It takes about fifty minutes to get there.

hǎi lún　chú le zuò gōng jiāo　hái yǒu bié de fāng shì ma
海伦：除了坐公交，还有别的方式吗？

Helen: Is there any other way to get there besides by bus?

ān nà　nǐ yě kě yǐ chéng zuò dì tiě　zài xiǎo dōng mén xià
安娜：你也可以乘坐地铁，在小东门下。

Anna: You can also take the subway and get off at Xiao Dong Men station.

hǎi lún　hǎo de　wǒ míng bai le　xiè xie nǐ
海伦：好的，我明白了，谢谢你。

Helen: OK, I see, thank you.

ān nà　bù kè qi
安娜：不客气。

Anna: You are welcome.

cí huì 词汇　Vocabulary

huáng hè lóu 黄鹤楼　*noun*　the Yellow Crane Tower

zhī dào 知道　*verb*　know

chéng zuò 乘坐　*verb*　take

gōng jiāo 公交　*noun*　bus

fāng shì 方式　*noun*　way

dì tiě 地铁　*noun*　subway

xiè xie 谢谢　*phrase*　thank you

míng bai 明白　*verb*　see

课后习题
Exercises

1. 根据拼音写出汉字。

Write the corresponding Chinese characters according to the syllables.

rú hé(　　　　)　　　　dǎ rǎo(　　　　)

qǐng wèn(　　　　)　　　　zhī dào(　　　　)

2. 用所给词语造句。

Make sentences according to the given words.

(1)大概

____

(2)乘坐

____

(3)需要

____

3. 根据课文完成句子。

Fill in the sentences according to the text.

(1)还有别的(　　　)吗?

(2)你也可以(　　　)地铁。

4. 英译汉。

English-Chinese Translation.

(1)It takes about fifty minutes to get there.

____

(2)Is there any other way to get there besides by bus?

____

5. 将下列词语组成句子。

Make sentences with the following words.

(1)请问 去 黄鹤楼 怎么

____

(2)方式 还有 交通 别的 吗

____

6. 听写

Dictation.

18. 设置中文输入法 (shè zhì zhōng wén shū rù fǎ)

dà wèi xiǎng qǐng nǐ bāng xià máng kě yǐ ma
大卫：想请你帮下忙可以吗？

ōu wén dāng rán kě yǐ shén me shì
欧文：当然可以，什么事？

dà wèi wǒ yào gěi lǎo shī jiāo yī fèn zuò yè dàn wǒ bù huì gěi diàn nǎo shè zhì zhōng wén shū rù fǎ
大卫：我要给老师交一份作业，但我不会给电脑设置中文输入法。

18. Setting Chinese input method

David：May I ask you for a favor?

Owen：Sure. What's the matter?

David： I should hand in an assignment to my teacher. But I can't set the Chinese input method for my computer.

ōu wén zhè méi nà me má fan wǒ bāng nǐ shǒu xiān dǎ kāi shè zhì diǎn jī shū rù nǐ jiāng huì zài zuǒ shàng fāng kàn dào bìng qiě zài zuǒ xià fāng yǒu de biāo zhì diǎn jī biāo zhì dǎ kāi nǐ jiāng huì zài píng mù de shàng miàn bù fen kàn dào zuì hòu xuǎn zé zhōng wén shū rù

欧文：这没那么麻烦，我帮你。首先，打开“设置”，点击“输入”，你将会在左上方看到“ABC”，并且在左下方有“＋”的标志，点击“＋”标志。打开 Microsoft word file，你将会在屏幕的上面部分看到“A”，最后选择中文输入。

Owen：It's not that troublesome. I'll help you. First, open the Settings and click the Input. You will see “ABC” on the upper left, and the sign of “＋” on the lower left. Click the “＋” sign, open a Microsoft word file, and you will see “A” on the upper part of the screen. Finally, select Chinese input.

dà wèi ò hǎo de xiè xie nǐ

大卫：哦，好的。谢谢你。

David：Oh, well, thank you.

ōu wén bù kè qi

欧文：不客气。

Owen：You're welcome.

cí huì

词汇 Vocabulary

diàn nǎo 电脑 *noun* computer

shè zhì 设置 *verb* set

zhōng wén 中文 *noun* Chinese

shū rù 输入 *verb* input

má fan 麻烦 *adjective* troublesome

biāo zhì 标志 *noun* sign

píng mù 屏幕 *noun* screen

xuǎn zé 选择 *verb* select

课后习题
Exercises

1. 根据拼音写出汉字。

Write the corresponding Chinese characters according to the syllables.

diàn nǎo(　　　　)　　　　zhōng wén(　　　　)

shè zhì(　　　　)　　　　shū rù(　　　　)

2. 用所给词语造句。

Make sentences according to the given words.

(1)电脑

____

(2)点击

____

(3)屏幕

____

3. 根据课文完成句子。

Fill in the sentences according to the text.

(1)想请你(　　　　)可以吗?

(2)最后选择(　　　　)输入。

4. 英译汉。

English-Chinese Translation.

(1)How to set the Chinese input method on the computer?

____

(2)It's not that troublesome. I'll help you.

____

5. 将下列词语组成句子。

Make sentences with the following words.

(1)要　老师　给　作业　一份　我　交

____

(2)打开　点击　首先　设置　输入

____

6. 听写

Dictation.

19. 滴滴打车 (dī dī dǎ chē)

19. Didi Dache

hǎi lún wǒ xiǎng qù shāng chǎng nǐ zhī dào zěn me yòng shǒu jī dǎ chē ma
海伦：我想去商场，你知道怎么用手机打车吗？

Helen：I want to go to the mall. Do you know how to take a taxi by mobile phone?

dà wèi zhī dào nǐ yòng de shì shén me pái zi de shǒu jī
大卫：知道，你用的是什么牌子的手机？

David：Yes. What brand of the mobile phone are you using?

hǎi lún píng guǒ shǒu jī
海伦：苹果手机。

Helen：iPhone.

dà wèi shǒu xiān nǐ yào qù yìng yòng shāng diàn xià zǎi dī dī dǎ chē
大卫：首先，你要去应用商店下载滴滴打车。

David：First，you need to go to the App Store to download Didi Dache.

hǎi lún hǎo de xià zǎi hǎo le rán hòu ne
海伦：好的，下载好了。然后呢？

Helen：Okay，it's downloaded，and then?

dà wèi dǎ kāi yìng yòng rán hòu tā huì zì dòng dìng wèi nǐ de chéng chē dì diǎn 大卫：打开应用，然后它会自动定位你的乘车地点。	David: Open the app and it'll automatically locate your pick-up point.
hǎi lún duì yǐ jīng zì dòng shí bié le 海伦：对，已经自动识别了。	Helen: Yeah, it's automatically identified.
dà wèi zuì hòu shū rù nǐ yào qù de dì diǎn diǎn jī dǎ chē 大卫：最后，输入你要去的地点，点击打车。	David: Finally, input your destination and click the button of "Request Taxi".
hǎi lún hǎo de wǒ zhī dào le xiè xie nǐ 海伦：好的，我知道了，谢谢你。	Helen: OK, I see. Thank you.

cí huì 词汇 / Vocabulary

dǎ chē 打车	*verb* take a taxi
xià zǎi 下载	*verb* download
yìng yòng 应用	*noun* application
zì dòng 自动	*adverb* automatically
shí bié 识别	*verb* identify
shū rù 输入	*verb* input

课后习题
Exercises

1. 根据拼音写出汉字。

Write the corresponding Chinese characters according to the syllables.

dǎ chē(　　　)　　　　xià zǎi(　　　)

yìng yòng(　　　)　　　　zì dòng(　　　)

2. 用所给词语造句。

Make sentences according to the given words.

(1)商场

____

(2)手机

____

(3)下载

____

3. 根据课文完成句子。

Fill in the sentences according to the text.

(1)你用的是(　　　)的手机?

(2)自动定位你的(　　　)地点。

4. 英译汉。

English-Chinese Translation.

(1)Do you know how to take a taxi by mobile phone?

____

(2)Open the app and it'll automatically locate your pick-up point.

____

5. 将下列词语组成句子。

Make sentences with the following words.

(1)知道　你　打车　怎么　手机　用　吗

____

(2)去　你要　的　地点　输入

____

6. 听写

Dictation.

cān tīng diǎn cān
20. 餐厅点餐

20. Ordering a meal in a restaurant

diàn yuán　nín hǎo　xū yào diǎn shén me
店员：您好，需要点什么？

Clerk: Hello, what would you like to order?

zhāng wěi　yǒu shén me tuī jiàn de ma
张伟：有什么推荐的吗？

Zhang Wei: What do you recommend?

diàn yuán　wǒ men diàn de jī tāng hé chǎo fàn dōu hěn bù cuò
店员：我们店的鸡汤和炒饭都很不错。

Clerk: The chicken soup and fried rice in our restaurant are both very good.

zhāng wěi　nà xiān lái ge jī tāng ba　rán hòu zài yào yī fèn ròu sī chǎo fàn
张伟：那先来个鸡汤吧，然后再要一份肉丝炒饭。

Zhang Wei: I'd like to have chicken soup first, and then a bowl of fried rice with shredded pork.

diàn yuán hǎo de qǐng nín xiān jiù zuò mǎ shàng gěi nín shàng cài 店员：好的，请您先就座，马上给您上菜。	Clerk: OK, please take your seat first. Your food will be served at once.
chī wán fàn hòu （吃完饭后）	(After the meal)
zhāng wěi nǐ hǎo wǒ yào jié zhàng 张伟：你好，我要结账。	Zhang Wei: Hello, I'd like to have the check.
diàn yuán hǎo de yī fèn tāng hé yī wǎn chǎo fàn yī gòng yuán zhī fù bǎo hái shì wēi xìn 店员：好的，一份汤和一碗炒饭，一共20元。支付宝还是微信？	Clerk: OK. A portion of soup and a bowl of fried rice, 20 yuan altogether. Alipay or WeChat?
zhāng wěi zhī fù bǎo 张伟：支付宝。	Zhang Wei: Alipay.
diàn yuán hǎo de xiè xie huì gù 店员：好的。谢谢惠顾。	Clerk: OK, thanks for your patronage.

cí huì 词汇 / Vocabulary

cān tīng 餐厅	*noun* restaurant
diǎn cān 点餐	*verb* order
tuī jiàn 推荐	*verb* recommend
jī tāng 鸡汤	*noun* chicken soup
ròu sī 肉丝	*noun* shredded meat
chǎo fàn 炒饭	*noun* fried rice

jiù zuò
就 座 *verb* take your seat

jié zhàng
结 账 *verb* have the check

zhī fù bǎo
支 付 宝 *noun* Alipay

wēi xìn
微 信 *noun* WeChat

课 后 习 题
Exercises

1. 根据拼音写出汉字。

Write the corresponding Chinese characters according to the syllables.

cān tīng (　　　)　　diǎn cān (　　　)

tuī jiàn (　　　)　　jī tāng(　　　)

2. 用所给词语造句。

Make sentences according to the given words.

(1)就座

____

(2)餐厅

____

(3)结账

____

3. 根据课文完成句子。

Fill in the sentences according to the text.

(1)有什么(　　　)的吗?

(2)马上给您(　　　)。

4. 英译汉。

English-Chinese Translation.

(1) I would like to have chicken soup first.

____

(2) OK, please take your seat first. Your food will be served at once.

____

5. 将下列词语组成句子。

Make sentences with the following words.

(1)什么　有　吗　推荐的

____

(2)给　马上　您　上菜

____

6. 听写

Dictation.

dìng jī piào **21. 定 机 票**	**21. Booking an air ticket**
qián tái　nín hǎo　yǒu shén me xū yào ma 前 台：您 好，有 什 么 需 要 吗？	Receptionist: Hello, may I help you?
lǐ hào　wǒ xiǎng yù dìng yī zhāng xià zhōu rì sì yuè yī rì běi jīng dào shàng hǎi de jī piào 李 浩：我 想 预 订 一 张 下 周 日 四 月 一 日 北 京 到 上 海 的 机 票。	Li Hao: I'd like to book a ticket from Beijing to Shanghai next Sunday, April 1st.
qián tái　qǐng shāo děng　wǒ lái bāng nín chá yī xià 前 台：请 稍 等。我 来 帮 您 查 一 下。	Receptionist: Wait a moment, please. Let me check it for you.

lǐ hào wǒ xiǎng dìng shāng wù cāng ér qiě zuì hǎo shì zǎo shàng de háng bān
李浩：我想订商务舱，而且最好是早上的航班。

Li Hao: I'd like to book business class, and I prefer a morning flight.

qián tái guó háng cì háng bān zǎo shàng jiǔ diǎn sān shí fēn qǐ fēi
前台：国航 CA1519 次航班，早上九点三十分起飞。

Receptionist: Air China flight CA1519 takes off at 9:30 a. m.

lǐ hào wǒ yìng gāi jǐ diǎn dào jī chǎng bǐ jiào hé shì
李浩：我应该几点到机场比较合适？

Li Hao: What time is the suitable time for me to arrive at the airport?

qián tái qī diǎn sān shí fēn kāi shǐ yàn piào
前台：七点三十分开始验票。

Receptionist: The check-in begins at 7:30.

lǐ hào hǎo de nà wǒ huì qī diǎn zhōng dào jī chǎng
李浩：好的，那我会七点钟到机场。

Li Hao: OK, then I will be at the airport at seven o'clock.

qián tái nín yǒu xíng li xū yào tuō yùn ma
前台：您有行李需要托运吗？

Receptionist: Do you have any luggage to consign?

lǐ hào wǒ yǒu liǎng gè xiāng zi xū yào tuō yùn
李浩：我有两个箱子需要托运。

Li Hao: I have two pieces of luggage to consign.

qián tái zhè shì suí shēn xíng li hé tuō yùn xíng li de yǒu guān guī dìng qǐng tián xiě nín de xiāng guān xìn xī
前台：这是随身行李和托运行李的有关规定。请填写您的相关信息。

Receptionist: Here are the rules for carry-on and checked luggage. Please fill in your information.

lǐ hào hǎo de xiè xie
李浩：好的，谢谢。

Li Hao: OK, thanks.

词汇 (cí huì) Vocabulary

预定 (yù dìng)	*verb*	book
机票 (jī piào)	*noun*	air ticket
商务 (shāng wù)	*noun*	business
航班 (háng bān)	*noun*	flight
规定 (guī dìng)	*noun*	rule
起飞 (qǐ fēi)	*verb*	take off
合适 (hé shì)	*adjective*	suitable
验票 (yàn piào)	*verb*	check-in
行李 (xíng li)	*noun*	luggage
托运 (tuō yùn)	*verb*	consign
信息 (xìn xī)	*noun*	information

课后习题
Exercises

1. 根据拼音写出汉字。

Write the corresponding Chinese characters according to the syllables.

yù dìng (　　　　)　　　　jī piào (　　　　)

shāng wù (　　　　)　　　　háng bān (　　　　)

2. 用所给词语造句。

Make sentences according to the given words.

(1)规定

____

(2)起飞

____

(3)合适

____

3. 根据课文完成句子。

Fill in the sentences according to the text.

(1)请(　　)。我来帮您查一下。

(2)我(　　　　)几点到(　　　　)比较合适?

4. 英译汉。

English-Chinese Translation.

(1) The check-in begins at 7:30.

____

(2) I have two pieces of luggage to check.

____

5. 将下列词语组成句子。

Make sentences with the following words.

(1)有　您　托运　吗　需要　行李

____

(2)填写　信息　相关　请　的　您

____

6. 听写

Dictation.

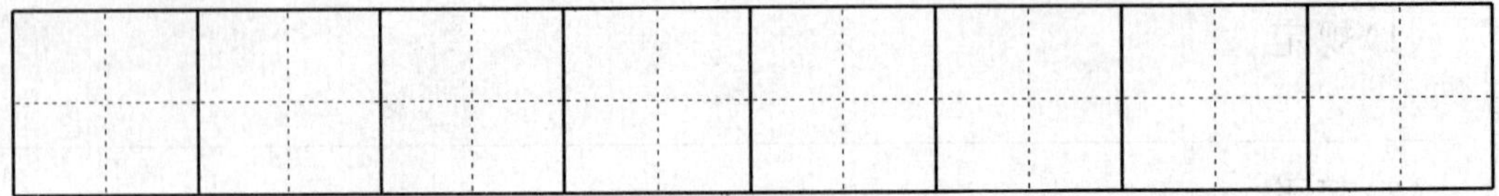

jì kuài dì
22. 寄快递

wú fāng nǐ hǎo wǒ xiǎng yào jì kuài dì
吴芳：你好，我想要寄快递。

yuán gōng hǎo de nín yào jì shén me
员工：好的，您要寄什么？

wú fāng wǒ xiǎng jì yī bù shǒu jī dào guǎng zhōu
吴芳：我想寄一部手机到广州。

yuán gōng hǎo de wǒ men zhè lǐ shǒu zhòng shì měi gōng jīn yuán xù zhòng shì měi gōng jīn yuán
员工：好的，我们这里首重是每公斤12元，续重是每公斤5元。

wú fāng méi wèn tí
吴芳：没问题。

yuán gōng qǐng chū shì nín de shēn fèn zhèng zài zhè zhāng biǎo shàng tián xiě xìng míng hé diàn huà hào mǎ děng xìn xī
员工：请出示您的身份证，在这张表上填写姓名和电话号码等信息。

22. Sending a package

Wu Fang: Hello, I want to send a package.

Staff: OK, what do you want to send?

Wu Fang: I want to send a mobile phone to Guangzhou.

Staff: OK. The first weight is 12 yuan/kg, and the additional weight is 5 yuan/kg.

Wu Fang: No problem.

Staff: Please show me your identification card and fill in your name, phone number and other information on this form.

wú fāng tián hǎo le gěi nǐ shén me shí hòu néng dào ne 吴芳：填好了，给你。什么时候能到呢？	Wu Fang: OK, here it is. When will the package arrive?
yuán gōng liǎng sān tiān zuǒ yòu 员工：两三天左右。	Staff: About two or three days.
wú fāng hǎo de wǒ zhī dào le xiè xie 吴芳：好的，我知道了，谢谢。	Wu Fang: I see. Thank you.

cí huì 词汇　　Vocabulary

kuài dì 快递	*noun* send a package (express delivery)
yuán gōng 员工	*noun* staff
shǒu jī 手机	*noun* mobile phone
méi wèn tí 没问题	*phrase* no problem
chū shì 出示	*verb* show
shēn fèn zhèng 身份证	*noun* identification card
tián xiě 填写	*verb* fill in
xìng míng 姓名	*noun* name
diàn huà hào mǎ 电话号码	*noun* phone number
zuǒ yòu 左右	*adverb* about

课后习题
Exercises

1. 根据拼音写出汉字。

Write the corresponding Chinese characters according to the syllables.

kuài dì (　　　　)　　　　yuán gōng(　　　　)

shǒu jī (　　　　)　　　　chū shì(　　　　)

2. 用所给词语造句。

Make sentences according to the given words.

(1)身份证

____

(2)填写

____

(3)电话

____

3. 根据课文完成句子。

Fill in the sentences according to the text.

(1)我想要寄(　　　)。

(2)我们这里(　　　)是每公斤 12 元。

4. 英译汉。

English-Chinese Translation.

(1)What do you want to send?

____

(2)Please show me your identification card.

____

5. 将下列词语组成句子。

Make sentences with the following words.

(1)时候 能 什么 到

---

(2)上 表 信息 张 填写 在 这

---

6. 听写

Dictation.

23. 旅行 (lǚ xíng)

23. Travel

hǎi lún hēi nǐ shì yào qù lǚ xíng ma
海伦：嗨，你是要去旅行吗？

Helen: Hi, are you going to travel?

ān nà duì wǒ qù shàng hǎi kàn wǒ mèi mei mèi fu hái yǒu wài sheng nǚ tā yǐ jīng shàng xiǎo xué èr nián jí le
安娜：对，我去上海看我妹妹、妹夫，还有外甥女。她已经上小学二年级了。

Anna: Yes, I will go to Shanghai to visit my younger sister, younger brother-in-law and my niece. My niece is already in Grade 2 in primary school.

hǎi lún nǐ shì zuò huǒ chē qù hái shì zuò fēi jī qù
海伦：你是坐火车去还是坐飞机去？

Helen: Will you travel by train or by plane?

ān nà wǒ zuò gāo tiě qù
安娜：我坐高铁去。

Anna: I will travel by high-speed railway.

hǎi lún zhēn de ma wǒ hái méi zuò guò
海伦：真的吗？我还没坐过。

Helen: Really? I've never been on a high-speed railway.

ān nà wǒ huì zuò lǚ xíng de xiǎo shì pín huí lái le gěi nǐ kàn
安娜：我会做旅行的小视频，回来了给你看。

Anna: I will make a travel vlog and show you after coming back.

hǎi lún nǐ jǐ diǎn chū fā
海伦：你几点出发？

Helen: What's your departure time?

ān nà liǎng xiǎo shí hòu
安娜：两小时后。

Anna: 2 hours later.

hǎi lún wǒ jīn tiān bù máng wǒ sòng nǐ qù chē zhàn ba
海伦：我今天不忙，我送你去车站吧。

Helen: I am not busy today. I can take you to the station.

ān nà zhēn de ma má fan nǐ le
安娜：真的吗？麻烦你了。

Anna: Really? Sorry to bother you.

hǎi lún bù má fan zhèng hǎo wǒ huí lái de shí hòu qù tàng chāo shì
海伦：不麻烦，正好我回来的时候去趟超市。

Helen: There's no problem. I can go to the supermarket on my way home.

ān nà xiè xie le
安娜：谢谢了。

Anna: Thank you.

cí huì 词汇 / Vocabulary

lǚ xíng
旅行 — *verb* travel

mèi mei
妹妹 — *noun* younger sister

mèi fu
妹夫 — *noun* younger brother-in-law

wài sheng nǚ
外甥女 — *noun* niece

xiǎo xué
小学 — *noun* primary school

huǒ chē 火车	*noun*	train
fēi jī 飞机	*noun*	plane
gāo tiě 高铁	*noun*	high-speed railway
shì pín 视频	*noun*	vlog (video log)
chē zhàn 车站	*noun*	station
má fan 麻烦	*verb*	bother
chāo shì 超市	*noun*	supermarket

课后习题
Exercises

1. 根据拼音写出汉字。

Write the corresponding Chinese characters according to the syllables.

lǚ xíng (　　　　)　　　　mèi mei (　　　　)

wài sheng nǚ (　　　　)　　　　xiǎo xué (　　　　)

2. 用所给词语造句。

Make sentences according to the given words.

(1)火车

____

(2)视频

____

(3)车站

____

3. 根据课文完成句子。

Fill in the sentences according to the text.

(1)你是要坐(　　　)去还是(　　　)去？

(2)我会做旅行的(　　　)。

4. 英译汉。

English-Chinese Translation.

(1)Hi, are you going to travel?

____

(2)I am not busy today. I can take you to the station.

____

5. 将下列词语组成句子。

Make sentences with the following words.

(1)出发　你　几点

____

(2)我　正好　的　超市　回来　趟　时候　去

____

6. 听写

Dictation.

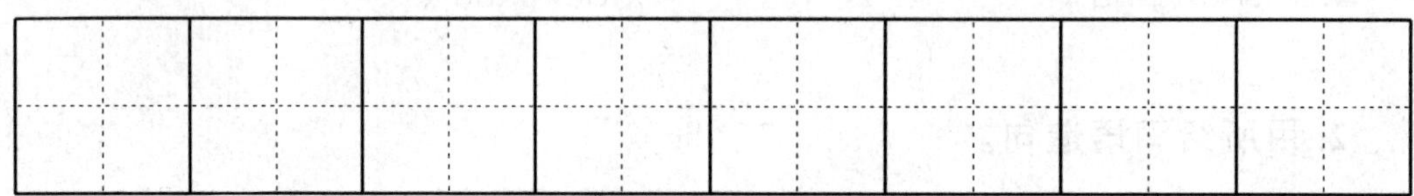

gòu wù

24. 购 物

24. Shopping

diàn yuán　zǎo shàng hǎo　nín xiǎng mǎi shén me

店 员：早 上 好，您 想 买 什 么？

Staff: Good morning, may I help you?

gù kè wǒ xiǎng mǎi yī jiàn shàng yī hé yī tiáo niú zǎi kù
顾客：我想买一件上衣和一条牛仔裤。

Customer: I want to buy a jacket and a pair of jeans.

diàn yuán nín kàn kan zhè jiàn zěn me yàng? hěn shì hé nín
店员：您看看这件怎么样？很适合您。

Staff: How about this one? It fits you.

gù kè wǒ bù xǐ huān hóng sè
顾客：我不喜欢红色。

Customer: I don't like red.

diàn yuán zhè jiàn hēi sè de nín jué de zěn me yàng
店员：这件黑色的您觉得怎么样？

Staff: How about this black one?

gù kè tǐng piào liang de
顾客：挺漂亮的。

Customer: That's nice.

diàn yuán zhè tiáo niú zǎi kù ne dā pèi zhè jiàn shàng yī hěn hǎo kàn
店员：这条牛仔裤呢？搭配这件上衣很好看。

Staff: And how about this pair of jeans? It's a good choice to collocate with the jacket.

gù kè zhè yī tào duō shǎo qián
顾客：这一套多少钱？

Customer: How much is this set?

diàn yuán yī gòng yuán
店员：一共1000元。

Staff: 1000 yuan in total.

gù kè tài guì le kě yǐ pián yi diǎn ma yuán zěn me yàng
顾客：太贵了，可以便宜点吗？800元怎么样？

Customer: It's too expensive. Can it be cheaper? How about 800 yuan?

diàn yuán hǎo de zhè shì zhǎo gěi nín de líng qián
店员：好的。这是找给您的零钱。

Staff: Fine. Here's your change.

gù kè xiè xie
顾客：谢谢。

Customer: Thank you.

cí huì 词汇 Vocabulary

gòu wù 购物	*noun*	shopping
shàng yī 上衣	*noun*	jacket
niú zǎi kù 牛仔裤	*noun*	jeans
shì hé 适合	*verb*	fit
hóng sè 红色	*noun*	red
hēi sè 黑色	*adjective*	black
piào liang 漂亮	*adjective*	nice
dā pèi 搭配	*verb*	collocate
pián yi 便宜	*adjective*	cheap
líng qián 零钱	*noun*	change

课后习题
Exercises

1. 根据拼音写出汉字。

Write the corresponding Chinese characters according to the syllables.

gòu wù (　　　　)　　　　shì hé(　　　　)

shàng yī (　　　　)　　　　hóng sè(　　　　)

2. 用所给词语造句。

Make sentences according to the given words.

(1)红色

____

(2)漂亮

---

(3)便宜

---

3. 根据课文完成句子。

Fill in the sentences according to the text.

(1)我想买(　　　)上衣和一条(　　　)。

(2)我不喜欢(　　　)。

4. 英译汉。

English-Chinese Translation.

(1)How about this one? It fits you.

---

(2)It's a good choice to collocate with the jacket.

---

5. 将下列词语组成句子。

Make sentences with the following words.

(1)一套　钱　多少　这

---

(2)挺　的　漂亮

---

6. 听写

Dictation.

bàn lǐ xìn yòng kǎ

25. 办理信用卡

ōu wén nǐ zhī dào zěn me bàn lǐ xìn yòng kǎ ma
欧文：你知道怎么办理信用卡吗？

ān nà zhī dào nǐ kě yǐ zài gè dà yín háng guān wǎng sōu suǒ xiáng xì xìn xī xiān xiǎng hǎo bàn nǎ zhǒng yín háng kǎ
安娜：知道，你可以在各大银行官网搜索详细信息，先想好办哪种银行卡。

ōu wén wǒ xiǎng xuǎn zé gōng shāng yín háng kǎ
欧文：我想选择工商银行卡。

ān nà nà nǐ kě yǐ qù zuì jìn de gōng shāng yín háng de yíng yè tīng shēn qǐng bàn lǐ
安娜：那你可以去最近的工商银行的营业厅申请办理。

ōu wén rán hòu ne
欧文：然后呢？

ān nà kāi tōng zhàng hù shōu dào kǎ de tóng shí huì yǒu xiāng guān de shǐ yòng zhǐ nán zǐ xì yuè dú jì zhù jié zhàng rì hé huán kuǎn rì tóng shí kě gēn jù tí shì shè zhì xiāng guān mì mǎ
安娜：开通账户，收到卡的同时会有相关的使用指南。仔细阅读，记住结账日和还款日，同时可根据提示设置相关密码。

ōu wén fēi cháng gǎn xiè zài jiàn
欧文：非常感谢，再见。

25. Applying for a credit card

Owen: Do you know how to get a credit card?

Anna: Yes. You can search the information in detail on official websites of all major banks, and first think about which bank card you want to get.

Owen: I want to choose ICBC.

Anna: Then you can apply for a card in the nearest ICBC business hall.

Owen: And then?

Anna: Open your account. Then you will get related guidebook when getting the credit card. Read carefully, remember the balance sheet date and repayment date. And you can also set the related password according to the prompt.

Owen: Thank you very much, goodbye.

ān nà zài jiàn
安娌：再见。

Anna: Bye.

cí huì
词汇

Vocabulary

xìn yòng kǎ 信用卡	*noun* credit card
yín háng 银行	*noun* bank
sōu suǒ 搜索	*verb* search
guān wǎng 官网	*noun* official website
zuì jìn de 最近的	*adjective* the nearest
yíng yè tīng 营业厅	*noun* business hall
kāi tōng 开通	*phrase* open one's account
shǐ yòng 使用	*verb* use
zhǐ nán 指南	*noun* guidebook
huán kuǎn 还款	*noun* repayment
shè zhì 设置	*verb* set
mì mǎ 密码	*noun* password

课后习题
Exercises

1. 根据拼音写出汉字。

Write the corresponding Chinese characters according to the syllables.

xìn yòng kǎ(　　　　)　　　　yín háng (　　　　)

sōu suǒ(　　　　)　　　　guān wǎng (　　　　)

2. 用所给词语造句。

Make sentences according to the given words.

(1)搜索

____

(2)开通

____

(3)使用

____

3. 根据课文完成句子。

Fill in the sentences according to the text.

(1)可以在各大(　　　)官网(　　　)详细信息

(2)你知道怎么(　　　)信用卡吗?

4. 英译汉。

English-Chinese Translation.

(1)Then you can apply for a card in the nearest ICBC business hall.

____

(2)Remember the balance sheet date and repayment date.

____

5. 将下列词语组成句子。

Make sentences with the following words.

(1)去　营业厅　最近的　申请　的　办理　可以

____

(2)相关　指南　阅读　使用　的

____

6. 听写

Dictation.

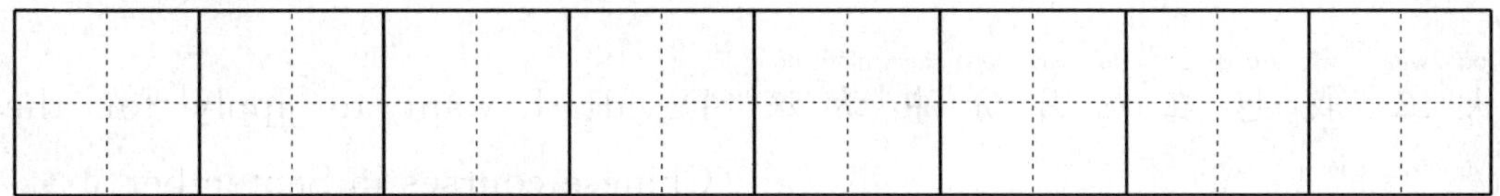

26. 申请奖学金 (shēn qǐng jiǎng xué jīn)

26. Applying for the scholarship

大卫(dà wèi)：嗨(hēi)，你(nǐ)最(zuì)近(jìn)过(guò)得(de)怎(zěn)么(me)样(yàng)？

David: Hi, how's it going?

安娜(ān nà)：还(hái)不(bù)错(cuò)，你(nǐ)呢(ne)？

Anna: Good. How about you?

大卫(dà wèi)：我(wǒ)也(yě)是(shì)，不(bù)过(guò)我(wǒ)在(zài)担(dān)心(xīn)一(yī)件(jiàn)事(shì)。

David: Me too. But I'm worried about one thing.

安娜(ān nà)：什(shén)么(me)事(shì)？

Anna: What is it?

大卫(dà wèi)：我(wǒ)想(xiǎng)留(liú)在(zài)中(zhōng)国(guó)深(shēn)造(zào)，但(dàn)不(bù)知(zhī)道(dào)怎(zěn)么(me)申(shēn)请(qǐng)。

David: I want to stay in China for further study, but I don't know how to apply.

安娜(ān nà)：你(nǐ)想(xiǎng)申(shēn)请(qǐng)哪(nǎ)个(gè)级(jí)别(bié)？

Anna: Which rank do you want to apply for?

dà wèi shuò shì xué wèi 大卫：硕士学位。	David：A master's degree.
ān nà zài zhōng guó yǒu liǎng zhǒng jiào xué fāng shì kě gòng shuò shì xuǎn zé，yīng yǔ de hé hàn yǔ de。yǒu guó jiā、shěng、jī gòu、qǐ yè、wài guó děng lèi bié de jiǎng xué jīn。 安娜：在中国有两种教学方式可供硕士选择，英语的和汉语的。有国家、省、机构、企业、外国等类别的奖学金。	Anna：There are two kinds of teaching methods provided for masters. One is in English，the other is in Chinese. There are national，provincial，institutional，enterprise，foreign and other types of scholarships.
dà wèi wǒ xiǎng zài jiǔ yuè fèn shēn qǐng hàn yǔ kè chéng 大卫：我想在九月份申请汉语课程。	David：I want to apply for the Chinese courses in September.
ān nà nà me nǐ xū yào zhǔn bèi jiǎng xué jīn shēn qǐng biǎo、dà xué shēn qǐng biǎo、jīng gōng zhèng de shēn zào wén píng jí chéng jì dān、xué xí jì huà shū、liǎng fèn tuī jiàn shū、guó wài tǐ jiǎn biǎo、wú fàn zuì jì lù zhèng míng hé yǒu xiào hù zhào 安娜：那么你需要准备奖学金申请表、大学申请表、经公证的深造文凭及成绩单、学习计划书、两份推荐书、国外体检表、无犯罪记录证明和有效护照。	Anna：Then you need to prepare a scholarship application form，a university application form，a notarized postgraduate diploma and a transcript，a study plan，two recommendation letters，a foreign medical examination form，a certificate of no criminal record and a valid passport.
dà wèi zhěng lǐ wán wén jiàn hòu，wǒ xià yī bù yīng gāi zuò shén me 大卫：整理完文件后，我下一步应该做什么？	David：After filing away，what should I do next?
ān nà qù wǎng zhàn shēn qǐng，shàng chuán zhè xiē wén jiàn hé nǐ de zhào piàn 安娜：去网站申请，上传这些文件和你的照片。	Anna：Apply on the website and upload these files and your photo.
dà wèi hǎo de，wǒ zhī dào le，xiè xie 大卫：好的，我知道了，谢谢。	David：OK，I got it. Thank you.

cí huì 词汇	Vocabulary
jiǎng xué jīn 奖学金	*noun* scholarship
shēn zào 深造	*noun* further study
jí bié 级别	*noun* rank
shuò shì 硕士	*noun* master's degree
zhèng fǔ 政府	*noun* government
jī gòu 机构	*noun* institution
qǐ yè 企业	*noun* enterprise
gōng zhèng 公证	*verb* notarize
wén píng 文凭	*noun* diploma
tǐ jiǎn 体检	*noun* medical examination
hù zhào 护照	*noun* passport
zhěng lǐ 整理	*verb* file away

课后习题

Exercises

1. 根据拼音写出汉字。

Write the corresponding Chinese characters according to the syllables.

jiǎng xué jīn (　　　　)　　　　shēn zào (　　　　)

jí bié (　　　　)　　　　shuò shì (　　　　)

2. 用所给词语造句。

Make sentences according to the given words.

(1)政府

______

(2)护照

______

(3)整理

______

3. 根据课文完成句子。

Fill in the sentences according to the text.

(1)你(　　　)过得(　　　)?

(2)(　　　)我在(　　　)一件事。

4. 英译汉。

English-Chinese Translation.

(1)How to apply for the scholarship?

______

(2)What is it?

______

5. 将下列词语组成句子。

Make sentences with the following words.

(1)想　我　深造　中国　留　在

______

(2)这些　你　文件　上传　照片　的　和

______

6. 听写

Dictation.

miàn shì

27. 面试

lǐ hào nín hǎo

李浩：您好。

miàn shì guān nǐ hǎo qǐng zuò qǐng jiǎn dān jiè shào yī xià nǐ zì jǐ

面试官：你好，请坐。请简单介绍一下你自己。

lǐ hào wǒ jiào lǐ hào wǒ yī zhí dōu duì jì suàn jī chéng xù gǎn xìng qù bìng qiě cóng shì guò diàn nǎo zhù lǐ de gōng zuò

李浩：我叫李浩。我一直都对计算机程序感兴趣，并且从事过电脑助理的工作。

miàn shì guān nǐ jué de zì jǐ yǒu shén me yōu diǎn

面试官：你觉得自己有什么优点？

lǐ hào wǒ xué dōng xi hěn kuài bìng qiě wǒ huì é yǔ yīng yǔ hàn yǔ sān mén yǔ yán rú guǒ guì gōng sī néng gěi wǒ yī gè jī huì wǒ yī dìng huì jié jìn suǒ néng wán chéng gōng zuò

李浩：我学东西很快，并且我会俄语、英语、汉语三门语言。如果贵公司能给我一个机会，我一定会竭尽所能完成工作。

27. Interview

Li Hao: Hello.

Interviewer: Hello, have a seat, please. Please briefly introduce yourself.

Li Hao: My name is Li Hao. I have always been interested in computer programs and worked as a computer assistant.

Interviewer: What strengths do you think you have?

Li Hao: I am a quick learner, and I can speak Russian, English and Chinese. If you can give me a chance, I will try my best to finish the job.

miàn shì guān hǎo de wǒ liǎo jiě le nǐ xiān huí qù ba miàn shì jié guǒ wǒ men huì tōng guò diàn huà gào zhī de 面试官：好的，我了解了。你先回去吧，面试结果我们会通过电话告知的。	Interviewer: OK, I get the picture. You go back first. We'll inform you of the result of the interview by phone.
lǐ hào hǎo de 李浩：好的。	Li Hao: OK.

cí huì 词汇 Vocabulary

miàn shì 面试	*noun* interview
jiè shào 介绍	*verb* introduce
chéng xù 程序	*noun* program
xìng qù 兴趣	*noun* interest
yōu diǎn 优点	*noun* strength
jié jìn suǒ néng 竭尽所能	*phrase* try one's best
gào zhī 告知	*verb* inform

课后习题
Exercises

1. 根据拼音写出汉字。

Write the corresponding Chinese characters according to the syllables.

miàn shì (　　　　)　　　　jiè shào (　　　　)

chéng xù (　　　　)　　　　　　xìng qù (　　　　)

2. 用所给词语造句。

Make sentences according to the given words.

(1)优点

____

(2)工作

____

(3)兴趣

____

3. 根据课文完成句子。

Fill in the sentences according to the text.

(1)请(　　　)一下你自己。

(2)并且(　　　)过电脑(　　　)的工作。

4. 英译汉。

English-Chinese Translation.

(1)What strengths do you think you have?

____

(2)I have always been interested in computer programs.

____

5. 将下列词语组成句子。

Make sentences with the following words.

(1)我　很　东西　学　快

____

(2)所能　我　会　一定　工作　竭尽　完成

____

6. 听写

Dictation.

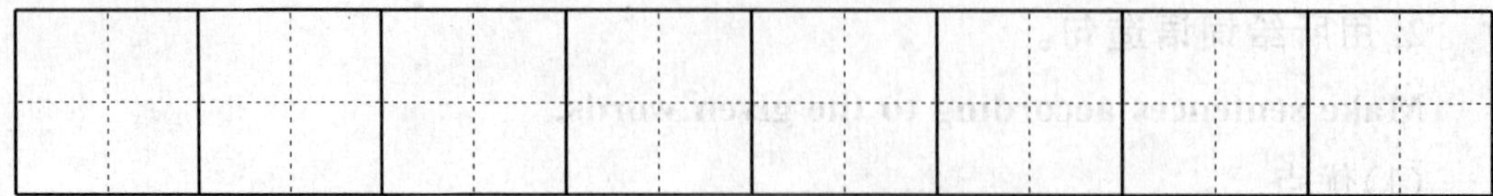

28. 学习中文的方法 (xué xí zhōng wén de fāng fǎ)

28. Ways to learn Chinese

hǎi lún: nǐ de zhōng wén hěn hǎo, kě yǐ gào sù wǒ nǐ de xué xí fāng fǎ ma?

海伦：你的中文很好，可以告诉我你的学习方法吗？

Helen: Your Chinese is very good. Could you tell me your learning method?

ān nà: dāng rán kě yǐ。zài shǒu jī zhōng shǐ yòng "Hanping Lite" hé "Pleco" děng cí diǎn。mǎi yī běn zhōng wén shū lái liàn xí nǐ de yuè dú hé xiě zuò néng lì。

安娜：当然可以。在手机中使用"Hanping Lite"和"Pleco"等词典。买一本中文书来练习你的阅读和写作能力。

Anna: Sure. Use "Hanping Lite", "Pleco" and other dictionaries on your phone. Buy a Chinese book to practice your reading and writing skills.

hǎi lún: wǒ zuì jìn gāng mǎi le yī běn zhōng wén shū。

海伦：我最近刚买了一本中文书。

Helen: I just bought a Chinese book recently.

ān nà: nǐ hái yào duō yǔ zhōng guó péng you jiāo liú, liàn xí nǐ de kǒu yǔ néng lì。wǒ hái huì zài qiáng bì shàng zhān tiē hàn zì hé pīn yīn tiē zhǐ。

安娜：你还要多与中国朋友交流，练习你的口语能力。我还会在墙壁上粘贴汉字和拼音贴纸。

Anna: You should also communicate with your Chinese friends to practice your oral Chinese. I also paste Chinese characters and pinyin stickers on the walls.

hǎi lún: nà kě zhēn shì gè hǎo zhǔ yi, xiè xie nǐ。

海伦：那可真是个好主意，谢谢你。

Helen: That's a good idea. Thank you.

cí huì 词汇 Vocabulary

fāng fǎ 方法	*noun*	method
cí diǎn 词典	*noun*	dictionary
liàn xí 练习	*verb*	practice
yuè dú 阅读	*noun*	reading
xiě zuò 写作	*noun*	writing
kǒu yǔ 口语	*adjective*	oral
néng lì 能力	*noun*	ability
qiáng bì 墙壁	*noun*	wall
zhān tiē 粘贴	*verb*	paste
tiē zhǐ 贴纸	*noun*	sticker

课后习题
Exercises

1. 根据拼音写出汉字。

Write the corresponding Chinese characters according to the syllables.

fāng fǎ (　　　　)　　　　cí diǎn (　　　　)

liàn xí (　　　　)　　　　yuè dú(　　　　)

2. 用所给词语造句。

Make sentences according to the given words.

(1)口语

____

(2)能力

____

(3)墙壁

____

3. 根据课文完成句子。

Fill in the sentences according to the text.

(1)(　　　)一本中文书来(　　　)你的阅读和写作(　　　)。

(2)我还会在(　　　)上(　　　)汉字和拼音(　　　)。

4. 英译汉。

English-Chinese Translation.

(1)That's a good idea. Thank you.

____

(2)Use "Hanping Lite" and "Pleco" on your phone.

____

5. 将下列词语组成句子。

Make sentences with the following words.

(1)你　学习　的　方法　我　告诉　可以　吗

____

(2)还要　多　朋友　你　与　中国　交流

____

6. 听写

Dictation.

29. 报名 HSK 考试

bào míng kǎo shì

dà wèi zǎo shàng hǎo
大卫：早上好。

ōu wén zǎo shàng hǎo nǐ de hàn yǔ kǎo shì zhǔn bèi de zěn me yàng
欧文：早上好。你的汉语考试准备得怎么样？

dà wèi wǒ zài zhǔn bèi cān jiā kǎo shì dàn bù zhī dào zěn me zhù cè nǐ zhī dào ma
大卫：我在准备参加 HSK 考试，但不知道怎么注册，你知道吗？

ōu wén zhī dào dǎ kāi hàn yǔ kǎo shì fú wù wǎng zhù cè chéng wéi wǎng zhàn yòng hù bào míng shí xuǎn zé kǎo shì xiàng mù rì qī dì diǎn tián xiě gè rén xìn xī àn wǎng yè shàng yāo qiú shàng chuán zì jǐ de diàn zǐ zhào piàn wán chéng kǎo shì yù yuē de kǎo shēng tōng guò dēng lù gè rén zhōng xīn chá kàn kǎo shì jì lù xuǎn zé zài xiàn zhī fù
欧文：知道。打开汉语考试服务网，注册成为网站用户，报名时选择考试项目、日期、地点，填写个人信息，按网页上要求上传自己的电子照片。完成考试预约的考生通过登录个人中心，查看“考试记录”，选择在线支付。

29. Registering for the HSK

David: Good morning.

Owen: Good morning. How are you preparing for your Chinese test?

David: I'm going to take the HSK exam. But I don't know how to register. Do you know?

Owen: Yes. Open the Chinese testing service website and register as a website user. Select the test item, date, and place during registration. Fill in your personal information and upload your electronic photo according to the requirements of the website. Candidates who complete the test reservation can log in the personal center to check the test record and choose to pay online.

dà wèi hǎo de wǒ liǎo jiě le xiè xie nǐ
大卫：好的，我了解了。谢谢你。

David：OK，I see. Thank you.

ōu wén bù kè qì
欧文：不客气。

Owen：You're welcome.

cí huì 词汇 Vocabulary

hàn yǔ 汉语	*noun*	Chinese
wǎng zhàn 网站	*noun*	website
xiàng mù 项目	*noun*	item
rì qī 日期	*noun*	date
dì diǎn 地点	*noun*	place
yù yue 预约	*noun*	reservation
zài xiàn 在线	*adjective*	online
liǎo jiě 了解	*verb*	see

课后习题 Exercises

1. 根据拼音写出汉字。

Write the corresponding Chinese characters according to the syllables.

hàn yǔ (　　　　)　　wǎng zhàn (　　　　)

xiàng mù (　　　　)　　rì qī (　　　　)

2. 用所给词语造句。

Make sentences according to the given words.

(1)地点

____

(2)准备

____

(3)注册

____

3. 根据课文完成句子。

Fill in the sentences according to the text.

(1)(　　　)汉语考试服务网,(　　　)成为网站(　　　)

(2)填写(　　　),按(　　　)上要求(　　　)自己的电子照片。

4. 英译汉。

English-Chinese Translation.

(1) How are you getting ready for your Chinese test?

____

(2) Open the Chinese testing service website and register as a website user

____

5. 将下列词语组成句子。

Make sentences with the following words.

(1)时　考试　选择　地点　报名　日期　和　项目

____

(2)记录　中心　个人　通过　查看　登录　考试

____

6. 听写

Dictation.

zhōu mò

30. 周末

dà wèi hēi nǐ shì chū qù wán le ma
大卫：嗨，你是出去玩了吗？

ōu wén shì de gāng cóng dōng hú huí lái,
hé péng you men zài nà lǐ wán de hěn
kāi xīn
欧文：是的，刚从东湖回来，和朋友们在那里玩得很开心。

dà wèi nǐ men zài nà lǐ zuò le shén me
大卫：你们在那里做了什么？

ōu wén wǒ men zài hú biān sàn bù hái yī
qǐ chī le shāo kǎo
欧文：我们在湖边散步，还一起吃了烧烤。

dà wèi wa tīng qǐ lái hěn yǒu qù hé nǐ
men yī qǐ de dōu shì āi jí rén ma
大卫：哇，听起来很有趣，和你们一起的都是埃及人吗？

ōu wén bù shì yǒu é luó sī rén wū zī
bié kè rén hái yǒu měng gǔ rén
欧文：不是，有俄罗斯人、乌兹别克人，还有蒙古人。

dà wèi nà nǐ men shì zěn me jiāo liú de
大卫：那你们是怎么交流的？

30. Weekends

David: Hey, did you go out to play?

Owen: Yes. I just came back from East Lake. I had a good time there with my friends.

David: What did you do there?

Owen: We walked by the lakeside and had a barbecue together.

David: Wow, that sounds interesting. Were people with you all Egyptians?

Owen: No, there were Russians, Uzbeks and Mongolians.

David: So how did you communicate?

ōu wén　wǒ men yòng yīng yǔ gōu tōng
欧文：我们用英语沟通。

Owen: We communicated in English.

dà wèi　yǒu jī huì de huà kě yǐ bǎ nǐ de péng you jiè shào gěi wǒ rèn shí ma
大卫：有机会的话可以把你的朋友介绍给我认识吗？

David: Would you please introduce your friends to me if there is a chance?

ōu wén　dāng rán kě yǐ, xià cì wǒ men chū qù wán de shí hou nǐ yě yī qǐ lái ba
欧文：当然可以，下次我们出去玩的时候你也一起来吧。

Owen: Sure. When next time we go out, you can come, too.

dà wèi　hǎo, nà jiù yuē hǎo le
大卫：好，那就约好了。

David: OK, it's a deal.

cí huì
词汇

Vocabulary

zhōu mò
周末　*noun*　weekend

hú biān
湖边　*noun*　lakeside

sàn bù
散步　*verb*　walk around

shāo kǎo
烧烤　*noun*　barbecue

āi jí rén
埃及人　*noun*　Egyptian

é luó sī rén
俄罗斯人　*noun*　Russian

wū zī bié kè rén
乌兹别克人　*noun*　Uzbek

měng gǔ rén
蒙古人　*noun*　Mongolian

gōu tōng
沟通　*verb*　communicate

课后习题
Exercises

1. 根据拼音写出汉字。

Write the corresponding Chinese characters according to the syllables.

zhōu mò (　　　　)　　　　hú biān (　　　　)
sàn bù (　　　　)　　　　shāo kǎo (　　　　)

2. 用所给词语造句。

Make sentences according to the given words.

(1)散步

____

(2)湖边

____

(3)沟通

____

3. 根据课文完成句子。

Fill in the sentences according to the text.

(1)你是(　　　　)玩了吗?

(2)你们在(　　　　)做了(　　　　)?

4. 英译汉。

English-Chinese Translation.

(1)We walked around the lake and had a barbecue together.

____

(2)Wow, that sounds interesting. Were people with you all Egyptians?

____

5. 将下列词语组成句子。

Make sentences with the following words.

(1)交流 你们 怎么 是 的

______

(2)的 朋友 你 可以 我 介绍 给 吗

______

6. 听写

Dictation.

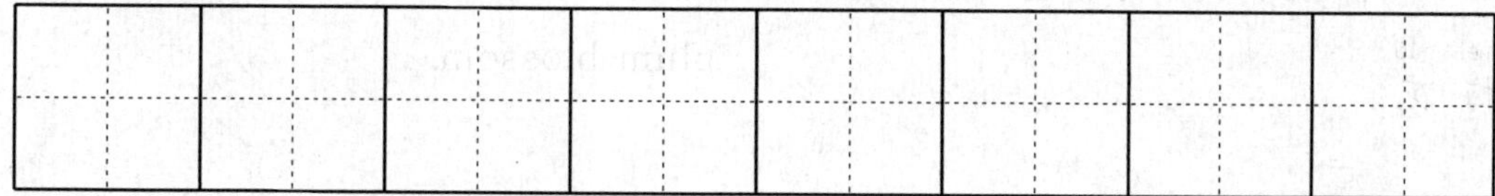

31. 梅花 (méi huā)

31. Plum blossom

海伦：嗨，早上好。(hǎi lún: hēi zǎo shàng hǎo)

Helen: Hey, good morning.

安娜：早上好！今天的天气真好，路边的花也开了。(ān nà: zǎo shàng hǎo jīn tiān de tiān qì zhēn hǎo lù biān de huā yě kāi le)

Anna: Good morning! The weather is nice, and the flowers by the side of the road are also in bloom.

海伦：对啊。要不我们一起去公园吧？(hǎi lún: duì a yào bù wǒ men yī qǐ qù gōng yuán ba)

Helen: Yes. How about going to the park together?

安娜：好呀！(ān nà: hǎo ya)

Anna: OK!

海伦：你知道梅花吗？(hǎi lún: nǐ zhī dào méi huā ma)

Helen: Do you know plum blossom?

安娜：不知道。你能给我讲讲吗？(ān nà: bù zhī dào nǐ néng gěi wǒ jiǎng jiǎng ma)

Anna: I don't know. Can you tell me?

hǎi lún méi huā yī bān zài dōng tiān kāi fàng zài zhōng guó chuán tǒng wén huà zhōng méi huā jì jiān qiáng yòu qiān xū jīng cháng jī lì zhe rén men
海伦：梅花一般在冬天开放。在中国传统文化中，梅花既坚强又谦虚，经常激励着人们。

Helen: Plum trees usually blossom in winter. In the traditional Chinese culture, plum blossom is both strong and modest and always encourages people.

ān nà wa wǒ zhēn xiǎng qù kàn kan méi huā
安娜：哇，我真想去看看梅花。

Anna: Wow, I really want to see plum blossom.

hǎi lún míng nián dōng tiān wǒ men yī qǐ qù kàn méi huā zěn me yàng
海伦：明年冬天我们一起去看梅花怎么样？

Helen: Next winter, how about going to see plum blossom together?

ān nà hǎo ya
安娜：好呀！

Anna: OK!

cí huì 词汇 Vocabulary

gōng yuán 公园 — *noun* park

méi huā 梅花 — *noun* plum blossom

jiān qiáng 坚强 — *adjective* strong

qiān xū 谦虚 — *adjective* modest

jī lì 激励 — *verb* encourage

míng nián 明年 — *noun* next year

课后习题

Exercises

1. 根据拼音写出汉字。

Write the corresponding Chinese characters according to the syllables.

méi huā(　　　　)　　　　tiān qì(　　　　)

gōng yuán(　　　　)　　　　jiān qiáng(　　　　)

wén huà(　　　　)　　　　dōng tiān(　　　　)

2. 用所给词语造句。

Make sentences according to the given words.

(1)明年

____

(2)激励

____

(3)谦虚

____

3. 根据课文完成句子。

Fill in the sentences according to the text.

(1)梅花一般在(　　　　)开放。

(2)要不我们一起去(　　　　)吧?

(3)在中国传统(　　　　)中,梅花既(　　　　)又(　　　　),经常(　　　　)着人们。

4. 英译汉。

English-Chinese Translation.

(1) I really want to see plum blossom.

____

(2) The flowers by the side of the road are also in bloom.

____

(3) Next winter, how about going to see plum blossom together?

____

5. 将下列词语组成句子。

Make sentences with the following words.

(1)梅花　你　吗　知道

____

(2)公园　去　我们　吧　一起

____

(3)天气　今天　真好　的

____

6. 听写

Dictation.

32. 太极

tài jí

dà wèi zǎo shàng hǎo
大卫：早上好！

ōu wén zǎo nǐ shì yào qù chén liàn ma
欧文：早！你是要去晨练吗？

dà wèi shì de wǒ zhǔn bèi qù dǎ tài jí quán nǐ yào yī qǐ qù ma
大卫：是的，我准备去打太极拳。你要一起去吗？

32. Tai Chi

David: Good morning!

Owen: Morning! Are you going to do morning exercise?

David: Yes, I'm going to play Tai Chi. Would you like to go together?

ōu wén tài jí quán shì shén me
欧文：太极拳是什么？

Owen: What is Tai Chi?

dà wèi tài jí quán shì zhōng guó wǔ shù de yī zhǒng kě yǐ qiáng shēn jiàn tǐ
大卫：太极拳是中国武术的一种，可以强身健体。

David: Tai Chi is a kind of Chinese kung fu that can keep fit.

ōu wén wǒ yě xiǎng xué kě yǐ jiāo wǒ ma
欧文：我也想学，可以教我吗？

Owen: I want to learn, too. Can you teach me?

dà wèi kě yǐ ya nà wǒ xiān jiāo nǐ dì yī gè dòng zuò
大卫：可以呀，那我先教你第一个动作。

David: Of course. I will teach you the first action.

ōu wén zhè gè dòng zuò hǎo xiàng bào zhe yī gè qiú a
欧文：这个动作好像抱着一个球啊。

Owen: It's like holding a ball.

dà wèi duì jiù shì zhè yàng zhè kě yǐ duàn liàn píng héng lì
大卫：对，就是这样，这可以锻炼平衡力。

David: Yeah, that's it. It can exercise the balance.

ōu wén wǒ jué de yǒu diǎn nán
欧文：我觉得有点难。

Owen: I feel it a little difficult.

dà wèi jiān chí zhù màn màn shì yìng jiù hǎo le duō duàn liàn nǐ de shēn tǐ yě huì biàn hǎo de
大卫：坚持住，慢慢适应就好了。多锻炼你的身体也会变好的。

David: Hold on and get used to it. You can be healthier by doing exercise.

ōu wén nǐ shuō de duì xiè xie nǐ jiāo wǒ tài jí
欧文：你说的对，谢谢你教我太极。

Owen: You are right. Thank you for teaching me Tai Chi.

词汇（cí huì） Vocabulary

太极 tài jí	*noun* Tai Chi
晨练 chén liàn	*noun* morning exercise
准备 zhǔn bèi	*verb* prepare
锻炼 duàn liàn	*verb* exercise
平衡 píng héng	*noun* balance
坚持 jiān chí	*verb* hold on
适应 shì yìng	*verb* get used to
教 jiāo	*verb* teach
难 nán	*adjective* difficult

课后习题
Exercises

1. 根据拼音写出汉字。

Write the corresponding Chinese characters according to the syllables.

chén liàn(　　　　)　　zhǔn bèi(　　　　)

wǔ shù(　　　　)　　dòng zuò(　　　　)

duàn liàn(　　　　)　　píng héng(　　　　)

2. 用所给词语造句。

Make sentences according to the given words.

(1)准备

____

(2)坚持

____

(3)适应

____

3. 根据课文完成句子。

Fill in the sentences according to the text.

(1)你是要去(　　　　)吗?

(2)我准备去打(　　　　　)。你要一起去吗?

(3)我也想(　　),可以(　　)我吗?

4. 英译汉。

English-Chinese Translation.

(1) I felt it a little difficult.

____

(2) You are right.

____

(3) I'm going to play Tai Chi. Would you like to go together?

____

5. 将下列词语组成句子。

Make sentences with the following words.

(1)是　什么　太极拳

____

(2)你　先　我　动作　第一个　教

____

(3)平衡　可以　这　锻炼

____

6. 听写

Dictation.

cháng chéng
33. 长　城

33. The Great Wall

hǎi lún nǐ hǎo nǐ zhōu mò zhǔn bèi gàn má
海伦：你好！你周末准备干嘛？

Helen: Hello! What are you going to do on the weekend?

dà wèi zhè zhōu mò wǒ xiǎng qù cān guān cháng chéng nǐ zhī qián qù guò cháng chéng ma
大卫：这周末我想去参观长城。你之前去过长城吗？

David: I want to visit the Great Wall this weekend. Have you ever been to the Great Wall before?

hǎi lún wǒ qù guò jǐ cì cháng chéng zhēn de fēi cháng xióng wěi zhuàng guān bù kuì shì shì jiè qī dà qí jì zhī yī
海伦：我去过几次。长城真的非常雄伟壮观，不愧是世界七大奇迹之一。

Helen: I have been to the Great Wall several times. It is magnificent. It deserves to be one of the seven wonders of the world.

dà wèi nǐ zhī dào cháng chéng de xiāng guān zhī shi ma
大卫：你知道长城的相关知识吗？

David: Do you know something about the Great Wall?

hǎi lún dāng rán zhī dào cháng chéng shì yī
海伦：当然知道。长城是一
xì liè fáng yù gōng shì mù dì shì bǎo hù
系列防御工事，目的是保护
zhōng huá dì guó dǐ kàng jūn shì rù qīn
中华帝国，抵抗军事入侵。
yī xiē chéng qiáng zǎo zài gōng yuán qián shì
一些城墙早在公元前7世
jì jiù kāi shǐ xiū jiàn zhè xiē chéng qiáng hòu
纪就开始修建，这些城墙后
lái lián jiē zài yī qǐ biàn dé gèng cháng gèng
来连接在一起，变得更长更
jiān gù xiàn zài tǒng chēng wéi cháng chéng
坚固，现在统称为长城。

Helen: Of course. The Great Wall of China is a series of fortifications and aims to protect the Chinese Empire and resist the military incursions. Several walls were built in as early as the 7th century BC. These, later joined together and made longer and stronger, are now collectively referred to as the Great Wall.

dà wèi wǒ yǐ jīng pò bù jí dài qù cān
大卫：我已经迫不及待去参
guān cháng chéng le
观长城了！

David: I can't wait to visit the Great Wall!

hǎi lún zhù nǐ zhōu mò wán de kāi xīn
海伦：祝你周末玩得开心！

Helen: Have a nice weekend!

cí huì
词汇

Vocabulary

cháng chéng
长城 *noun* the Great Wall

zhōu mò
周末 *noun* weekend

cān guān
参观 *verb* visit

xióng wěi zhuàng guān
雄伟壮观 *adjective* magnificent

dāng rán
当然 *adverb* of course

xiū jiàn
修建 *verb* build

mù dì
目的 *noun* target

课后习题
Exercises

1. 根据拼音写出汉字。

Write the corresponding Chinese characters according to the syllables.

cháng chéng(　　　　)　　cān guān(　　　　)

xióng wěi(　　　　)　　zhuàng guān(　　　　)

qí jì(　　　　)　　zhī shi(　　　　)

2. 用所给词语造句。

Make sentences according to the given words.

(1)周末

____

(2)目的

____

(3)参观

____

3. 根据课文完成句子。

Fill in the sentences according to the text.

(1)这(　　　　)我想去(　　　　)长城。

(2)你(　　　　)长城的相关(　　　　)吗?

(3)祝你周末玩得(　　　　)!

4. 英译汉。

English-Chinese Translation.

(1) What are you going to do on the weekend?

____

(2) I have been to the Great Wall several times.

____

(3) The Great Wall of China is a series of fortifications.

____

5. 将下列词语组成句子。

Make sentences with the following words.

(1)去过　长城　吗　你

____

(2)参观　了　迫不及待　我　已经　长城　去

____

(3)不愧　是　长城　世界　之一　七大奇迹

____

6. 听写

Dictation.

34. 黄鹤楼 (huáng hè lóu)

34. The Yellow Crane Tower

hé mā ma dǎ diàn huà tán lùn huáng hè lóu
(和妈妈打电话谈论黄鹤楼)

(Talk about the Yellow Crane Tower on the phone with Mom.)

wǒ mā ma zǎo shàng hǎo wǒ xiàn zài zài cān guān huáng hè lóu
我：妈妈，早上好！我现在在参观黄鹤楼！

Me: Good morning, Mom! I am visiting the Yellow Crane Tower!

mā ma zhēn bàng nǐ néng gěi mā ma jiè shào yī xià huáng hè lóu ma
妈妈：真棒，你能给妈妈介绍一下黄鹤楼吗？

Mom: Cool. Can you tell me something about the Yellow Crane Tower?

wǒ dāng rán kāi qǐ shì pín tōng huà 我：当然。（开启视频通话）	Me: Of course. (Turning on video calling)
wǒ huáng hè lóu shì zhōng guó chuán tǒng jiàn zhù wèi yú zhōng guó wǔ hàn tā zài bù tóng de cháo dài yǒu bù tóng de jiàn zhù tè sè jīn tiān chù lì de zhè zuò lóu chóng jiàn yú nián jī yú qīng dài de shè jì tā gāo mǐ yuē yīng chǐ yǒu wǔ céng 我：黄鹤楼是中国传统建筑，位于中国武汉。它在不同的朝代有不同的建筑特色。今天矗立的这座楼重建于1981年，基于清代的设计。它高51.4米（约169英尺），有五层。	Me: The Yellow Crane Tower is a traditional Chinese building located in Wuhan, China. The tower had different architectural features in different dynasties. The tower which stands today is based on the one designed during the Qing dynasty, rebuilt in 1981. It is 51.4 meters high (about 169 feet) and it has 5 floors.
wǒ wú lùn cóng nǎ gè fāng xiàng kàn lóu de wài guān dōu shì yī yàng de wū dǐng fù gài zhe wàn kuài huáng sè liú lí wǎ huáng sè de wū yán cháo shàng měi céng lóu de shè jì dōu xiàng yī zhī huáng hè zhǎn kāi chì bǎng fēi xiáng 我：无论从哪个方向看，楼的外观都是一样的。屋顶覆盖着10万块黄色琉璃瓦。黄色的屋檐朝上，每层楼的设计都像一只黄鹤展开翅膀飞翔。	Me: The appearance of the tower is the same regardless of the direction it is viewed from. The roof is covered by 100,000 yellow glazed tiles. With upturned yellow eaves, each floor seems to have been designed to resemble a yellow crane spreading its wings to fly.
mā ma tài bàng le zhēn gāo xìng nǐ néng xué dào zhè me duō zhī shi 妈妈：太棒了！真高兴你能学到这么多知识。	Mom: That's great! I am glad that you have learned so much.

cí huì
词汇 — Vocabulary

huáng hè lóu 黄鹤楼	*noun* the Yellow Crane Tower

cān guān 参 观	*verb*　visit
chóng jiàn 重 建	*verb*　rebuild
jī yú 基 于	*verb*　base on
huáng sè 黄 色	*adjective*　yellow
shè jì 设 计	*noun*　design
wū dǐng 屋 顶	*noun*　roof
wū yán 屋 檐	*noun*　eave
chì bǎng 翅 膀	*noun*　wing

课后习题
Exercises

1. 根据拼音写出汉字。

Write the corresponding Chinese characters according to the syllables.

tán lùn(　　　　)　　jiè shào(　　　　)

dāng rán(　　　　)　　chuán tǒng(　　　　)

shè jì　(　　　　)　　chì bǎng　(　　　　)

2. 用所给词语造句。

Make sentences according to the given words.

(1)重建

____

(2)屋顶

____

(3)黄色

____

3. 根据课文完成句子。

Fill in the sentences according to the text.

(1)我现在在参观(　　　　　　　)!

(2)(　　　　　)覆盖着10万块(　　　　　)琉璃瓦。

(3)每层楼的(　　　　　)都像一只黄鹤展开(　　　　　)飞翔。

4. 英译汉。

English-Chinese Translation.

(1) Can you tell me something about the Yellow Crane Tower?

____

(2) The Yellow Crane Tower is a traditional Chinese building located in Wuhan, China.

____

(3) I am glad that you have learned so much.

____

5. 将下列词语组成句子。

Make sentences with the following words.

(1)1981年　黄鹤楼　于　重建

____

(2)塔　这　是　清代　座　设计的　基于

____

(3)我　打电话　妈妈　给　黄鹤楼　介绍

____

6. 听写

Dictation.

hú běi měi shí
35. 湖北美食

dà wèi nǐ wǔ fàn zhǔn bèi chī shén me
大卫：你午饭准备吃什么？

ōu wén wǒ hái méi xiǎng hǎo nǐ yǒu shén me hǎo chī de tuī jiàn ma
欧文：我还没想好。你有什么好吃的推荐吗？

dà wèi wǔ hàn yǒu hěn duō hǎo chī de wǒ zhī dào de jiù yǒu rè gān miàn zhōu hēi yā xiǎo lóng xiā děng děng
大卫：武汉有很多好吃的。我知道的就有热干面、周黑鸭、小龙虾，等等。

ōu wén rè gān miàn hěn shòu huān yíng ma wǒ zài wǔ hàn jīng cháng tīng shuō tā
欧文：热干面很受欢迎吗？我在武汉经常听说它。

dà wèi shì de rè gān miàn jì bù tóng yú liáng miàn yòu bù tóng yú tāng miàn tā shì zhǔ shú zhī hòu zài pèi tiáo liào de shì zài wǔ hàn chī zǎo cān de shǒu xuǎn xiǎo chī bù guò chī wán yǒu xiē gān duì le zhōu hēi yā yě bù cuò
大卫：是的，热干面既不同于凉面，又不同于汤面，它是煮熟之后再配调料的，是在武汉吃早餐的首选小吃，不过吃完有些干。对了，周黑鸭也不错。

35. Hubei Food

David: What are you going to have for lunch?

Owen: I have no idea. Do you have any delicious food to recommend?

David: There are many delicious foods in Wuhan. I know hot dry noodles, Zhou Black Duck, crayfish, and so on.

Owen: Are hot dry noodles very popular? I often hear about them in Wuhan.

David: Yes, they're different from cold noodles with sauce and noodles with soup. They are mixed with seasonings after being boiled. They are the preferred snack for breakfast in Wuhan, but you'll feel thirsty after eating. By the way, Zhou Black Duck is also very great.

ōu wén wǒ yě tīng shuō guò zhōu hēi yā hěn duō rén xǐ huān chī 欧文：我也听说过周黑鸭，很多人喜欢吃。	Owen: I've also heard about Zhou Black Duck. Many people like it very much.
dà wèi què shí hěn bù cuò, hěn là dàn shì hěn hǎo chī. zhè shì gè lián suǒ pǐn pái, ān quán wèi shēng, hěn kě kào 大卫：确实很不错，很辣但是很好吃。这是个连锁品牌，安全卫生，很可靠。	David: That's true. It tastes spicy, but it is really delicious. It's a chain brand, safe, healthful and reliable.
ōu wén wǒ yǐ jīng pò bù jí dài yào shì shì le 欧文：我已经迫不及待要试试了。	Owen: I can't wait to try it.
dà wèi nǐ kěn dìng huì ài shàng zhè lǐ de shí wù de, yīn wéi zhēn de tài měi wèi le. wǒ men xiàn zài jiù qù chī fàn ba 大卫：你肯定会爱上这里的食物的，因为真的太美味了。我们现在就去吃饭吧。	David: You will love the food here because it's really yummy. Let's have lunch now.
ōu wén hǎo a 欧文：好啊。	Owen: OK.

cí huì 词汇 / Vocabulary

wǔ fàn 午饭	*noun* lunch
hǎo chī 好吃	*adjective* delicious
shí wù 食物	*noun* food
là 辣	*adjective* spicy
jīng cháng 经常	*adverb* often

wèi shēng
卫 生 *adjective* healthful

xiàn zài
现 在 *adverb* now

课后习题
Exercises

1. 根据拼音写出汉字。

Write the corresponding Chinese characters according to the syllables.

tuī jiàn ( ) wǔ hàn ( )

huān yíng ( ) jīng cháng ( )

xiǎo chī ( ) xǐ huān ( )

2. 用所给词语造句。

Make sentences according to the given words.

(1)好吃

______

(2)现在

______

(3)经常

______

3. 根据课文完成句子。

Fill in the sentences according to the text.

(1)你( )准备吃什么？

(2)武汉有很多( )。

(3)我已经( )试试了。

4. 英译汉。

English-Chinese Translation.

(1) I have no idea.

____

(2) There are many delicious foods in Wuhan.

____

(3) Do you have any delicious food to recommend?

____

5. 将下列词语组成句子。

Make sentences with the following words.

(1)人　很多　吃　喜欢

____

(2)武汉人　早餐　是　吃　的　首选　这

____

(3)很　热干面　吗　欢迎　受

____

6. 听写

Dictation.

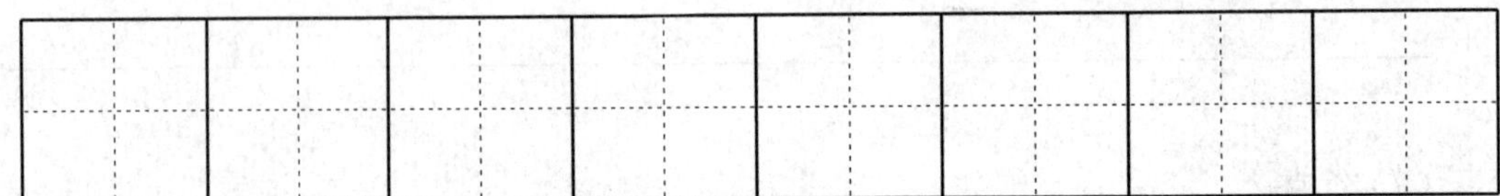

36. 中国书法 (zhōng guó shū fǎ)

36. Chinese calligraphy

安娜(ān nà)：嗨(hēi)，你(nǐ)最(zuì)近(jìn)在(zài)做(zuò)什(shén)么(me)？

Anna: Hi, what are you doing these days?

海伦(hǎi lún)：我(wǒ)在(zài)学(xué)习(xí)中(zhōng)国(guó)书(shū)法(fǎ)。

Helen: I am learning Chinese calligraphy.

ān nà nǐ wèi shén me xiǎng xué zhōng guó shū fǎ
安娜：你为什么想学中国书法？

Anna: Why do you want to learn Chinese calligraphy?

hǎi lún yīn wéi wǒ hěn xǐ huān zhōng guó shū fǎ de jì qiǎo hé fēng gé
海伦：因为我很喜欢中国书法的技巧和风格。

Helen: Because I like Chinese calligraphy skills and styles.

ān nà liàn xí zhōng guó shū fǎ xū yào nǎ xiē gōng jù
安娜：练习中国书法需要哪些工具？

Anna: What tools are needed to practice Chinese calligraphy?

hǎi lún xū yào bǐ mò zhǐ yàn
海伦：需要笔墨纸砚。

Helen: Writing brushes, ink sticks, paper and inkstone.

ān nà zhōng guó shū fǎ yǒu nǎ xiē fēng gé
安娜：中国书法有哪些风格？

Anna: What are the styles of Chinese calligraphy?

hǎi lún zhǔ yào yǒu wǔ zhǒng fēng gé zhuàn shū lì shū xíng shū cǎo shū kǎi shū
海伦：主要有五种风格：篆书、隶书、行书、草书、楷书。

Helen: It has five major styles: seal character, official script, running hand, cursive script and regular script.

ān nà kàn lái zhōng guó shū fǎ zhēn de lì shǐ yōu jiǔ a liàn xí shū fǎ yīng gāi hěn yǒu qù ba
安娜：看来中国书法真的历史悠久啊。练习书法应该很有趣吧！

Anna: It seems that Chinese calligraphy has a long history. It should be interesting to practice calligraphy.

hǎi lún shì de nǐ yào hé wǒ yī qǐ xué ma
海伦：是的，你要和我一起学吗？

Helen: Yes, would you like to join me?

ān nà hǎo a xiè xie
安娜：好啊，谢谢！

Anna: Of course, thank you!

词汇 cí huì　Vocabulary

书法 shū fǎ	*noun*	calligraphy
技巧 jì qiǎo	*noun*	skill
风格 fēng gé	*noun*	style
工具 gōng jù	*noun*	tool
有趣 yǒu qù	*adjective*	interesting

课后习题
Exercises

1. 根据拼音写出汉字。

Write the corresponding Chinese characters according to the syllables.

shū fǎ (　　)　　jì qiǎo (　　)

liàn xí (　　)　　gōng jù (　　)

bǐ(　　)　　yǒu qù (　　)

2. 用所给词语造句。

Make sentences according to the given words.

(1)学习

____

(2)练习

____

(3)需要

____

3. 根据课文完成句子。

Fill in the sentences according to the text.

(1)我很喜欢中国书法的(　　　　　)和(　　　　　)。

(2)练习书法需要的工具有(　　　　　　　　　　)。

(3)练习书法应该很(　　　　　)吧！

4. 英译汉。

English-Chinese Translation.

(1) What are you doing these days?

____

(2) Why do you want to learn Chinese calligraphy ?

____

(3) Because I like Chinese calligraphy skills and styles.

____

5. 将下列词语组成句子。

Make sentences with the following words.

(1)书法　在　我　学习

____

(2)要　你　我　一起　和　学习　吗

____

(3)风格　有　中国　哪些　书法

____

6. 听写

Dictation.

guó qìng jié
37. 国庆节

37. National Day

dà wèi nǐ zhī dào zhōng guó de guó qìng jié ma
大卫：你知道中国的国庆节吗？

David: Do you know Chinese National Day?

hǎi lún tīng shuō guò dàn wǒ hái méi yǒu qīn zì tǐ yàn guò nǐ zhī dào dà jiā zěn me guò guó qìng jié ma
海伦：听说过，但我还没有亲自体验过。你知道大家怎么过国庆节吗？

Helen: I have heard of it, but I have not experienced it. Do you know how people celebrate National Day?

dà wèi guó qìng jié shì fǎ dìng jié jià rì zài jià qī qī jiān hái huì yǒu xǔ duō qìng zhù huó dòng bǐ rú yān huā hé wǎn huì dà jiā hái huì lì yòng zhè gè jià qī lǚ xíng
大卫：国庆节是法定节假日，在假期期间还会有许多庆祝活动，比如烟花和晚会。大家还会利用这个假期旅行。

David: National Day is a statutory holiday, during which there are many celebrations, such as fireworks and evening parties. People will also take advantage of this holiday to travel.

hǎi lún nà zhēn shì tài hǎo le nǐ néng gěi wǒ jiǎng jiǎng guó qìng jié de lì shǐ ma
海伦：那真是太好了。你能给我讲讲国庆节的历史吗？

Helen: That's great. Can you tell me the history of Chinese National Day?

dà wèi zhōng huá rén mín gòng hé guó chéng lì yú nián yuè rì wèi le jì niàn guó jiā chéng lì měi nián yuè rì quán guó rén mín huān qìng guó qìng jié
大卫：中华人民共和国成立于1949年10月1日，为了纪念国家成立，每年10月1日全国人民欢庆国庆节。

David: The People's Republic of China was founded on October 1st, 1949. In order to commemorate the founding of the country, people across the country celebrate National Day on October 1st every year.

hǎi lún nǐ guó qìng jié zhǔn bèi zěn me dù guò
海伦：你国庆节准备怎么度过？

Helen: How will you spend your National Day?

dà wèi wǒ zhǔn bèi qù běi jīng lǚ yóu liáo jiě gèng duō zhōng guó lì shǐ wén huà
大卫：我准备去北京旅游，了解更多中国历史文化。

David: I'm going to travel to Beijing to learn more about Chinese history and culture.

hǎi lún zhēn hǎo zhù nǐ jià qī yú kuài
海伦：真好！祝你假期愉快！

Helen: Cool! Have a nice holiday!

cí huì 词汇 Vocabulary

guó qìng jié 国庆节	*noun*	National Day
tǐ yàn 体验	*verb*	experience
qìng zhù 庆祝	*verb*	celebrate
jià qī 假期	*noun*	holiday
huó dòng 活动	*noun*	activity
jì niàn 纪念	*verb*	commemorate
lǚ yóu 旅游	*verb*	travel
dù guò 度过	*verb*	spend
wén huà 文化	*noun*	culture

课后习题
Exercises

1. 根据拼音写出汉字。

Write the corresponding Chinese characters according to the syllables.

guó qìng jié (　　　　　)　　jié jià rì (　　　　　)

huó dòng (　　　　　)　　lì shǐ (　　　　　)

jì niàn (　　　　　)　　yú kuài (　　　　　)

2. 用所给词语造句。

Make sentences according to the given words.

(1)旅游

____

(2)活动

____

(3)纪念

____

3. 根据课文完成句子。

Fill in the sentences according to the text.

(1)在假期期间还会有许多(　　　　　)活动。

(2)大家还会(　　　　　)这个假期旅行。

(3)我想(　　　　　)更多中国历史文化。

4. 英译汉。

English-Chinese Translation.

(1) That's great!

____

(2) Do you know Chinese National Day?

____

(3) Have a nice holiday!

---

5. 将下列词语组成句子。

Make sentences with the following words.

(1)是　法定　国庆节　节假日

---

(2)亲自　还　我　体验　过　没有

---

(3)国庆节　你　怎么　准备　度过

---

6. 听写

Dictation.

38. 春节
chūn jié

xiǎo hóng　nǐ hǎo　wǒ shì xiǎo hóng　nǐ ne
小红：你好！我是小红，你呢？

mǎ lì　wǒ shì mǎ lì　lái zì yīng guó
玛丽：我是玛丽，来自英国。

hěn gāo xìng rèn shi nǐ　nǐ shì zhōng guó rén ma
很高兴认识你。你是中国人吗？

xiǎo hóng　shì de　zuì jìn zhōng guó zhèng zài huān dù chūn jié　nǐ zhī dào ma
小红：是的。最近中国正在欢度春节，你知道吗？

38. The Spring Festival

Xiao Hong: Hello! I'm Xiao Hong. What's your name?

Mary: My name is Mary. I'm from Britain. Nice to meet you. Are you Chinese?

Xiao Hong: Yes. Do you know that people in China are celebrating the Spring Festival recently?

mǎ lì wǒ tīng shuō guò chūn jié qǐng wèn
玛丽：我听说过春节。请问
chūn jié yǒu nǎ xiē xí sú ne
春节有哪些习俗呢？

Mary: I have heard about the Spring Festival. What are the customs of it?

xiǎo hóng yǐ qián de jiǎng jiu kě duō le xiàn
小红：以前的讲究可多了，现
zài jiù méi nà me duō le dàn jiā jiā hái
在就没那么多了，但家家还
shì yào tiē chūn lián chú xī yī jiā rén yào
是要贴春联，除夕一家人要
jù zài yī qǐ chī nián yè fàn yě jiào tuán
聚在一起吃年夜饭，也叫团
yuán fàn
圆饭。

Xiao Hong: There used to be a lot of traditions, but there aren't so many now. Each family still puts up Spring Festival couplets, and the whole family usually gather together for the family reunion dinner on New Year's Eve.

mǎ lì nián yè fàn dōu chī xiē shén me
玛丽：年夜饭都吃些什么？

Mary: What do you usually eat for the family reunion dinner?

xiǎo hóng nián yè fàn chī de hěn fēng shèng
小红：年夜饭吃得很丰盛，
jī yā yú ròu yī bān shì yī nián lǐ chī
鸡、鸭、鱼、肉，一般是一年里吃
de zuì hǎo de yī dùn le
得最好的一顿了。

Xiao Hong: The family reunion dinner is very abundant and includes chicken, duck, fish and meat, which is often the best meal for the whole year.

mǎ lì kàn lái chūn jié shì hé jiā tuán yuán
玛丽：看来春节是阖家团圆
de rì zǐ zhēn xìng fú ā
的日子.真幸福啊！

Mary: It seems that the Spring Festival is a time for family reunion. How happy it is!

xiǎo hóng shì de jīn tiān xià wǔ bù rú yī
小红：是的，今天下午不如一
qǐ qù wǒ jiā guò jié ba
起去我家过节吧.

Xiao Hong: Yes, why don't we go to my home for the holiday this afternoon?

mǎ lì hǎo ya xiè xie
玛丽：好呀，谢谢！

Mary: That's great. Thank you!

词汇 (cí huì) Vocabulary

chūn jié 春节	*noun*	the Spring Festival
xí sú 习俗	*noun*	custom
chūn lián 春联	*noun*	Spring Festival couplet
chú xī 除夕	*noun*	New Year's Eve
jī 鸡	*noun*	chicken
yā 鸭	*noun*	duck
yú 鱼	*noun*	fish
ròu 肉	*noun*	meat
tuán yuán 团圆	*verb*	reunion
xìng fú 幸福	*adjective*	happy

课后习题
Exercises

1. 根据拼音写出汉字。

Write the corresponding Chinese characters according to the syllables.

yīng guó ( ) rèn shi ( )

gāo xìng ( ) chūn jié ( )

xí sú ( ) tuán yuán ( )

2. 用所给词语造句。

Make sentences according to the given words.

(1)来自

____

(2)认识

____

(3)幸福

____

3. 根据课文完成句子。

Fill in the sentences according to the text.

(1)我是玛丽，来自(　　　　　)。

(2)以前的(　　　　　)可多了，现在就没有那么多了。

(3)年夜饭吃得很(　　　　　)。

4. 英译汉。

English-Chinese Translation.

(1) Are you Chinese?

____

(2) What do you usually eat for the family reunion dinner?

____

(3) What are the customs of the Spring Festival?

____

5. 将下列词语组成句子。

Make sentences with the following words.

(1)你　认识　很　高兴

____

(2)聚　一起　在　年夜饭　吃　一家人

____

(3)春节　欢度　最近　中国　正在

____

6. 听写

Dictation.

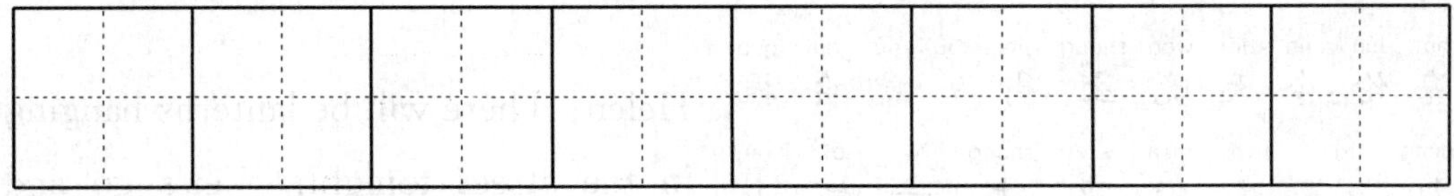

yuán xiāo jié

39. 元宵节

ān nà　yuán xiāo jié yào lái le　nǐ zhǔn bèi

安娜：元宵节要来了，你准备

zěn me dù guò yuán xiāo jié

怎么度过元宵节？

hǎi lún　dāng rán shì chī tāng yuán　guān dēng

海伦：当然是吃汤圆、观灯、

cāi dēng mí la

猜灯谜啦！

ān nà　tāng yuán shì shén me

安娜：汤圆是什么？

hǎi lún　tāng yuán yóu nuò mǐ hé dòu shā zuò

海伦：汤圆由糯米和豆沙做

chéng　xiàng zhēng zhe tuán tuán yuán yuán　hé jiā

成，象征着团团圆圆、阖家

xìng fú

幸福。

ān nà　nà wèi shén me yào guān dēng ne

安娜：那为什么要观灯呢？

hǎi lún　yuán xiāo jié diǎn dēng yīn wéi diǎn rán

海伦：元宵节点灯因为点燃

dēng huǒ yǒu zhào liàng qián chéng zhī yì　dà

灯火有照亮前程之意。大

jiā guān dēng de tóng shí hái huì yī tóng cāi

家观灯的同时还会一同猜

dēng mí

灯谜。

39. The Lantern Festival

Anna: The Lantern Festival is coming. How are you going to celebrate it?

Helen: Of course eat sweet dumplings, admire the lanterns and guess lantern riddles.

Anna: What are sweet dumplings?

Helen: Sweet dumplings are made of glutinous rice and bean paste, and they symbolize reunion and family happiness.

Anna: Then why do we admire the lanterns?

Helen: Lighting up lanterns on the Lantern Festival has the meaning of illuminating the future. While admiring the lanterns, people will also guess lantern riddles together.

ān nà wǒ zhī dào shén me shì cāi dēng mí 安娜：我知道什么是猜灯谜。 wǒ jué de cāi dēng mí kě yǒu yì sī le 我觉得猜灯谜可有意思了！	Anna: I know what guessing lantern riddles is. I think guessing lantern riddles is so interesting!
hǎi lún jīn tiān wǎn shàng jiē tóu jiù huì guà 海伦：今天晚上街头就会挂 dēng la wǒ men wǎn shàng yī qǐ qù 灯啦，我们晚上一起去 kàn ba 看吧！	Helen: There will be lanterns hanging in the street tonight. Let's go and admire them together then!
ān nà nà wǒ men fàng xué hòu jiù yī qǐ 安娜：那我们放学后就一起 qù ba 去吧！	Anna: Let's go together after school!

cí huì 词汇 — Vocabulary

yuán xiāo jié 元宵节	*noun*	the Lantern Festival
tāng yuán 汤圆	*noun*	sweet dumpling
nuò mǐ 糯米	*noun*	glutinous rice
dòu shā 豆沙	*noun*	bean paste
diǎn rán 点燃	*verb*	light up
qián chéng 前程	*noun*	career or future

课后习题

Exercises

1. 根据拼音写出汉字。

Write the corresponding Chinese characters according to the syllables.

tāng yuán ( ) cāi dēng mí ( )

nuò mǐ ( ) dòu shā ( )

wǎn shàng ( ) fàng xué ( )

2. 用所给词语造句。

Make sentences according to the given words.

(1)象征

____

(2)还

____

(3)一起

____

3. 根据课文完成句子。

Fill in the sentences according to the text.

(1)今天( )街头就会挂灯啦。

(2)( )灯火有( )前程之意。

(3)汤圆( )着团团圆圆、( )。

4. 英译汉。

English-Chinese Translation.

(1) The Lantern Festival is coming. How are you going to celebrate it?

____

(2) I think guessing lantern riddles is interesting.

____

(3) Let's go together after school.

---

5. 将下列词语组成句子。

Make sentences with the following words.

(1)习俗　元宵节　什么　有

---

(2)晚上　就会　今天　灯笼　街上　挂　了

---

(3)知道　什么　我　猜灯谜　是

---

6. 听写

Dictation.

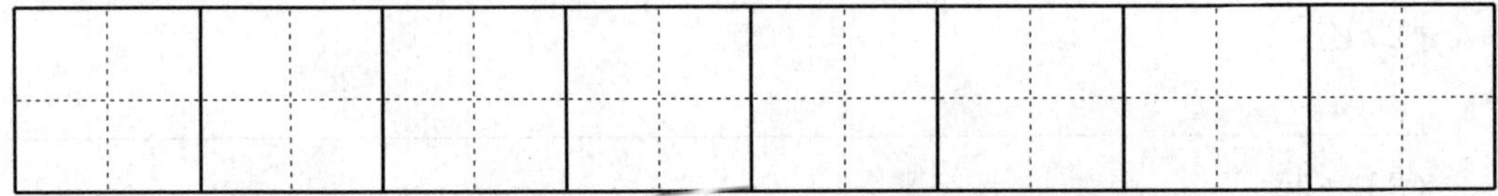

4.2 Articles

gōng fu
1. 功夫

gōng fu shì zhōng guó wǔ shù de sú chēng
功夫是中国武术的俗称。
zhōng guó wǔ shù de qǐ yuán kě yǐ zhuī sù
中国武术的起源可以追溯
dào zì wèi de xū yào shòu liè huó dòng yǐ
到自卫的需要、狩猎活动以
jí zhōng guó gǔ dài de jūn shì xùn liàn
及中国古代的军事训练。

gōng fu shì zhōng guó chuán tǒng tǐ yù yùn
功夫是中国传统体育运
dòng de yī zhǒng nián qīng rén hé lǎo nián rén
动的一种，年轻人和老年人
dōu liàn tā yǐ zhú jiàn yǎn biàn chéng le
都练。它已逐渐演变成了
zhōng guó wén huà de dú tè yuán sù
中国文化的独特元素。

gōng fu zuò wéi zhōng guó de guó bǎo yǒu
功夫作为中国的国宝，有
shàng bǎi zhǒng bù tóng de fēng gé shì shì jiè
上百种不同的风格，是世界
shàng liàn de zuì duō de wǔ shù xíng shì
上练得最多的武术形式。

1. Kung Fu

Chinese martial arts are commonly known as Kung Fu. The origin of Chinese martial arts can be traced back to the need of self-defence, hunting activities and military training in ancient China.

Kung Fu is one of the traditional sports in China, practiced by both the young and the old. It has gradually evolved into a unique element of Chinese culture.

As a national treasure of China, Kung Fu has hundreds of different styles and it is the most practiced martial art form in the world.

yǒu xiē fēng gé mó fǎng le dòng wù de dòng zuò, hái yǒu yī xiē zé shòu dào le zhōng guó zhé xué sī xiǎng、shén huà hé chuán shuō de qǐ fā.
有些风格模仿了动物的动作,还有一些则受到了中国哲学思想、神话和传说的启发。

Some styles imitate the movements of animals, while others are inspired by Chinese philosophy, myths and legends.

cí huì 词汇 | Vocabulary

sú chēng 俗称	*noun*	common name
qǐ yuán 起源	*noun*	origin
zhuī sù 追溯	*verb*	date from, trace back to
zì wèi 自卫	*noun*	self-defence
shòu liè 狩猎	*verb*	hunt
chuán tǒng 传统	*adjective*	traditional
zhú jiàn 逐渐	*adverb*	gradually
wén huà 文化	*noun*	culture
dú tè 独特	*adjective*	unique
fēng gé 风格	*noun*	style
xíng shì 形式	*noun*	form
bù tóng 不同	*adjective*	different

mó fǎng 模 仿	*verb*	imitate
dòng wù 动 物	*noun*	animal
zhé xué 哲 学	*noun*	philosophy
shén huà 神 话	*noun*	myth
chuán shuō 传 说	*noun*	legend
qǐ fā 启 发	*verb*	inspire

课后习题
Exercises

1. 请在括号里写出对应的拼音或汉字。

Please write down the right syllables or Chinese characters in the parentheses.

俗称(　　)　起源(　　)　追溯(　　)　自卫(　　)

狩猎(　　)　传统(　　)　逐渐(　　)　文化(　　)

dú tè(　　)　fēng gé(　　)　mó fǎng(　　)

dòng wù(　　)

2. 组词。

Combine words.

qǐ 起 {(　　) (　　)}　zhuī 追 {(　　) (　　)}　chuán 传 {(　　) (　　)}　mó 模 {(　　) (　　)}

3. 用下列所给词语组句。

Complete the sentences with the words given below.

(1)中国　是　功夫　俗称　的　武术。

____

(2)的　追溯　起源　武术　狩猎活动　可以　到。

____

(3)独特　文化　中国　元素　的　逐渐　已　它　演变　成了。

____

(4)风格　功夫　上百种　的　不同　有。

____

4. 提问或回答问题。

Ask or answer the questions.

(1)Q：中国武术的俗称是什么？

A：______________________________。

(2)Q：世界上练得最多的武术形式是什么？

A：______________________________。

(3)Q：______________________________？

A：有些风格模仿了动物的动作。

5. 翻译。

Translate.

(1)功夫是中国武术的俗称。

____

(2)它是中国传统体育运动的一种，年轻人和老年人都练。

____

(3)它已逐渐演变成了中国文化的独特元素。

____

(4)As a national treasure of China, Kung Fu has hundreds of different styles.

____

(5) It is the most practiced martial art form in the world.

____

6. 听写。

Dictation.

chá
2. 茶

zhōng guó shì yī gè wén huà lì shǐ yōu jiǔ
中国是一个文化历史悠久
de guó dù yě shì yī gè lǐ yí zhī bāng
的国度，也是一个礼仪之邦。
měi dāng kè rén lái fǎng dōu xū yào pào chá
每当客人来访，都需要泡茶
gěi kè rén hē
给客人喝。

zài gěi kè rén fèng chá zhī qián nǐ yīng gāi
在给客人奉茶之前，你应该
wèn wen tā men xǐ huan hē shén me lèi xíng
问问他们喜欢喝什么类型
de chá bìng cǎi yòng zuì hé shì de chá jù
的茶，并采用最合适的茶具
fèng shàng
奉上。

fèng chá qī jiān zhǔ rén xū yào zǐ xì liú
奉茶期间，主人需要仔细留
yì kè rén chá bēi lǐ de chá liàng
意客人茶杯里的茶量。

tōng cháng ruò shì yòng chá bēi pào chá zài chá
通常，若是用茶杯泡茶，在茶
hē wán yī bàn zhī hòu jiù yīng gāi jiā
喝完一半之后就应该加
kāi shuǐ
开水。

2. Tea

China is a country with time-honored civilization and also a state of courtesy and propriety. When guests visit, it is necessary to make tea for them.

Before serving tea, you should ask them what kind of tea they like, and serve them the tea with the most appropriate tea set.

During the course of serving tea, the host should keep an eye on the remaining tea in the guests' cups.

Usually, if the tea is made in a teacup, boiling water should be added into the cup when half of the tea has been consumed.

zhè yàng chá bēi jiù yī zhí dōu shì mǎn de
这样，茶杯就一直都是满的，
chá de fāng xiāng yě dé yǐ bǎo liú
茶的芳香也得以保留。

So, the cup is always full and the fragrance of tea remains.

cí huì 词汇 — Vocabulary

lì shǐ 历史	*noun* history
lǐ yí zhī bāng 礼仪之邦	*phrase* state of courtesy and propriety
kè rén 客人	*noun* guest
lái fǎng 来访	*verb* visit
pào chá 泡茶	*verb* make tea
lèi xíng 类型	*noun* type
chá jù 茶具	*noun* tea set
liú yì 留意	*verb* keep an eye on
tōng cháng 通常	*adverb* usually
yī bàn 一半	*noun* half
kāi shuǐ 开水	*noun* boiling water
fāng xiāng 芳香	*noun* fragrance
bǎo liú 保留	*verb* retain

课后习题
Exercises

1. 请在括号里写出对应的拼音或汉字。

Please write down the right syllables or Chinese characters in the parentheses.

历史（　　　） 礼仪（　　　） 客人（　　　） 来访（　　　）

泡茶（　　　） 类型（　　　） 茶具（　　　） 通常（　　　）

yí bàn（　　　） kāi shuǐ（　　　） fāng xiāng（　　　）

bǎo liú（　　　）

2. 组词。

Combine words.

fǎng 访（　　）（　　）　kè 客（　　）（　　）　bǎo 保（　　）（　　）　lái 来（　　）（　　）

3. 用下列所给词语组句。

Complete the sentences with the words given below.

(1)悠久　文化　的　历史　国度　是　中国　一个。

____

(2)问问　应该　你　都　他们　喝　类型　什么　喜欢　的　茶。

____

(3)需要　留意　仔细　客人　茶杯　的　主人　里　茶量。

____

(4)芳香　的　也　得以　茶　保留。

____

4. 提问或回答问题。

Ask or answer the questions.

(1)Q：______________________________?

A：中国是一个文化历史悠久的国家。

(2)Q：在给客人奉茶之前，你应该做些什么？

A：________________________________。

(3)Q：奉茶期间，主人需要干什么？

A：________________________________。

5. 翻译。

Translate.

(1)每当客人来访，都需要泡茶给客人喝。

____

(2)在给客人奉茶之前，你应该问问他们喜欢喝什么类型的茶。

____

(3)并采用最合适的茶具奉上。

____

(4)During the course of serving tea, the host should keep an eye on the remaining tea in the guests' cups.

____

(5)So, the cup is always full and the fragrance of tea is also retained.

____

6. 听写。

Dictation.

3. 春节 (chūn jié)

chūn jié shì zhōng guó rén mín zuì shèng dà de
春节是中国人民最盛大的
chuán tǒng jié rì rén men yòng gè zhǒng gè
传统节日。人们用各种各
yàng de xíng shì lái qìng zhù chūn jié
样的形式来庆祝春节，

3. The Spring Festival

The Spring Festival is the biggest traditional festival for the Chinese people. People use various forms to celebrate the Spring Festival,

bǐ rú fàng biān pào tiē chūn lián chī tuán nián fàn kàn wǔ shī shǎng huā dēng děng
比如放鞭炮，贴春联，吃团年饭，看舞狮，赏花灯等。

such as setting off firecrackers, pasting up Spring Festival couplets, having reunion dinners, watching the lion dance, admiring the lanterns, and so on.

bài nián shì chūn jié bù kě quē shǎo de yī xiàng huó dòng
拜年是春节不可缺少的一项活动，

Paying New Year calls is an indispensable activity of the Spring Festival,

yě shì rén men cí jiù yíng xīn xiāng hù biǎo dá měi hǎo zhù yuàn de yī zhǒng fāng shì
也是人们辞旧迎新、相互表达美好祝愿的一种方式。

and it is also a way for people to bid farewell to the old year and usher in the new, and express good wishes to each other.

zài chūn jié rén men dōu jìn kě néng de huí dào jiā lǐ hé qīn rén tuán jù biǎo dá duì wèi lái yī nián de rè qiè qī pàn hé duì xīn yī nián shēng huó de měi hǎo zhù fú
在春节，人们都尽可能地回到家里和亲人团聚，表达对未来一年的热切期盼和对新一年生活的美好祝福。

During the Spring Festival, people go home and get together with their relatives as much as possible to express their eager expectation for the coming year and good wishes for the New Year.

cí huì 词汇 Vocabulary

shèng dà
盛大 *adjective* grand

gè zhǒng gè yàng de
各种各样的 *adjective* various, all kinds of

biān pào
鞭炮 *noun* firecracker

tuán nián fàn
团年饭 *noun* reunion dinner

wǔ shī 舞 狮	*noun*	lion dance
huā dēng 花 灯	*noun*	lantern
qìng zhù 庆 祝	*verb*	celebrate
bǐ rú 比 如	*verb*	for example, such as
bù kě quē shǎo 不 可 缺 少	*adjective*	indispensable
xiāng hù 相 互	*adverb*	each other
zhù yuàn 祝 愿	*noun*	wish
jìn kě néng 尽 可 能	*adverb*	as much as possible
qīn rén 亲 人	*noun*	relative
tuán jù 团 聚	*verb*	reunite

课后习题

Exercises

1. 请在括号里写出对应的拼音或汉字。

Please write down the right syllables or Chinese characters in the parentheses.

春节（　　　）　盛大（　　　）　鞭炮（　　　）　春联（　　　）

团年饭（　　　）　舞狮（　　　）　花灯（　　　）　比如（　　　）

xiāng hù（　　　）　zhù yuàn（　　　）　qīn rén（　　　）　tuán jù（　　　）

2. 组词。

Combine words.

qīn 亲	( ) ( )	shèng 盛	( ) ( )	bài 拜	( ) ( )	nián 年	( ) ( )

3. 用下列所给词语组句。

Complete the sentences with the words given below.

(1)节日　传统　是　春节　中国　人民　盛大　最　的。

____

(2)用　人们　各种各样　形式　的　来　春节　庆祝。

____

(3)春节　拜年　是　不可缺少　的　活动　一项。

____

(4)尽可能地　人们　回到　都　和　家里　亲人　团聚。

____

4. 提问或回答问题。

Ask or answer the questions.

(1)Q：______________________________?

A：春节是中国人民最盛大的传统节目。

(2)Q：春节不可缺少的一项活动是什么?

A：______________________________。

(3)Q：在春节,人们都要干什么?

A：______________________________。

5. 翻译。

Translate.

(1)春节是中国人民最盛大的传统节日。

____

(2)人们用各种各样的形式来庆祝春节。

____

(3)拜年是春节不可缺少的一项活动。

___

(4)It is also a way for people to bid farewell to the old year and usher in the new, and express good wishes to each other.

___

(5)During the Spring Festival, people go home and get together with their relatives as much as possible.

___

6. 听写。

Dictation.

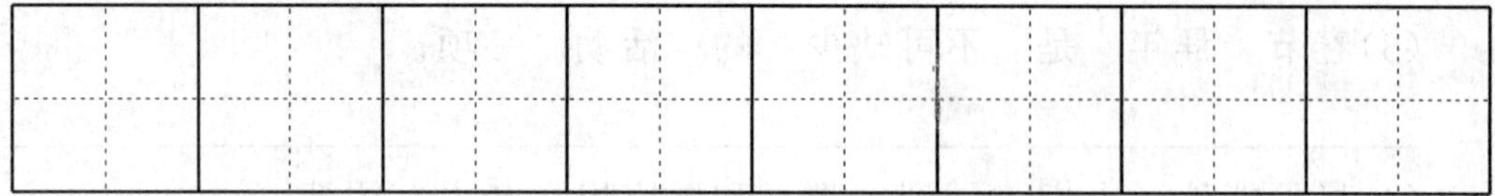

4. 生肖 (shēng xiào)

4. The Chinese zodiacs

生肖是中国传统文化的重要组成部分。它们源于自然界的11种动物和一个民族图腾。
(shēng xiào shì zhōng guó chuán tǒng wén huà de zhòng yào zǔ chéng bù fen. tā men yuán yú zì rán jiè de 11 zhǒng dòng wù hé yī gè mín zú tú téng.)

The Chinese zodiacs are an important part of Chinese traditional culture. They are derived from 11 animals in the nature and a national totem.

每个人都以其出生年的象征动物作为生肖，所以中国人常以生肖计算年龄。
(měi gè rén dōu yǐ qí chū shēng nián de xiàng zhēng dòng wù zuò wéi shēng xiào, suǒ yǐ zhōng guó rén cháng yǐ shēng xiào jì suàn nián líng.)

Each person uses his or her birth year's symbolic animal as a zodiac, so Chinese people usually use the zodiacs to calculate their ages.

shí èr shēng xiào fēn bié shì shǔ niú hǔ tù lóng shé mǎ yáng hóu jī gǒu zhū tā men dài biǎo de dòng wù xìng gé tè diǎn gè bù xiāng tóng
十二生肖分别是鼠、牛、虎、兔、龙、蛇、马、羊、猴、鸡、狗、猪，它们代表的动物性格特点各不相同。

The twelve Chinese zodiacs are rat, ox, tiger, rabbit, dragon, snake, horse, sheep, monkey, rooster, dog and pig. The animals they represent have different characteristics.

lì rú niú shì qín láo de xiàng zhēng tù dài biǎo zhe shàn liáng mǎ zé shì jī jí bù qū fú de dài biǎo
例如，牛是勤劳的象征；兔代表着善良；马则是积极、不屈服的代表。

For example, the ox is the symbol of diligence, and the rabbit represents goodness. The horse is the representative of positiveness and unyieldingness.

词汇 (cí huì) — Vocabulary

shēng xiào
生肖 — *noun* the Chinese zodiac

yuán yú
源于 — *verb* derive from

tú téng
图腾 — *noun* totem

dài biǎo
代表 — *verb* represent

xìng gé tè diǎn
性格特点 — *phrase* characteristic

jì suàn
计算 — *verb* calculate

qín láo
勤劳 — *adjective* diligent

xiàng zhēng
象征 — *noun* symbol

善良 (shàn liáng)	*noun*	goodness
积极 (jī jí)	*adjective*	positive
不屈服 (bù qū fú)	*adjective*	unyielding

课后习题
Exercises

1. 请在括号里写出对应的拼音或汉字。

Please write down the right syllables or Chinese characters in the parentheses.

生肖(　　) 源于(　　) 图腾(　　) 代表(　　)
性格(　　) 特点(　　) 计算(　　) 勤劳(　　)
xiàng zhēng(　　) shàn liáng(　　)
jī jí(　　) bù qū fú(　　)

2. 组词。

Combine words.

图 (tú) {(　　) (　　)} 特 (tè) {(　　) (　　)} 象 (xiàng) {(　　) (　　)} 源 (yuán) {(　　) (　　)}

3. 用下列所给词语组句。

Complete the sentences with the words given below.

(1)出生　年　每个　其　人　都　以　的　动物　生肖　作为　象征。

____

(2)代表　的　各不相同　他们　动物　性格特点。

____

(3)象征　是　勤劳　牛　的。

____

(4)代表　兔　善良　着。

____

4. 回答问题。

Answer the questions.

(1)Q：十二生肖源于什么？

A：______________________________。

(2)Q：人们把什么作为生肖？

A：______________________________。

(3)Q：马是什么品格的代表？

A：______________________________。

5. 翻译。

Translate.

(1)十二生肖是中国传统文化的重要组成部分。

____

(2)它们源于自然界的11种动物和一个民族图腾。

____

(3)每个人都以其出生年的象征动物作为生肖。

____

(4)The animals they represent have different characteristics.

____

(5)The horse is the representative of positiveness and unyieldingness.

____

6. 听写。

Dictation.
